Orchid Care

ORCHID CARE
A Guide to Cultivation and Breeding

Walter Richter

TRANSLATED AND ADAPTED BY DR EDMUND LAUNERT, F.L.S.
AND P. FRANCIS HUNT, M.SC.
LINE DRAWINGS BY HANS PREUSSE

VAN NOSTRAND REINHOLD COMPANY
NEW YORK   CINCINNATI   TORONTO   LONDON   MELBOURNE

First published in paperback in 1982
Copyright© 1969 by Neumann Verlag, Radebeul, GDR
English translation copyright© 1972 by Studio Vista Publishers,
London, U.K.
Library of Congress Catalog Card Number 76-29470

ISBN 0-442-26873-4

Van Nostrand Reinhold Company
135 West 50th Street, New York, NY 10020

Van Nostrand Reinhold Ltd.
1410 Birchmount Road, Scarborough, Ontario M1P 2E7

Van Nostrand Reinhold Australia Pty. Ltd.
17 Queen Street, Mitcham, Victoria 3132

Van Nostrand Reinhold Company Ltd.
Molly Millars Lane, Wokingham, Berkshire, England RG11 2PY

English-language cloth edition published 1977 by
Van Nostrand Reinhold Company
German edition published 1969 under the title *orchideen pflegen—
vermehren—züchten* by Neumann Verlag

16 15 14 13 12 11 10 9 8 7 6 5 4 3 2 1

CONTENTS

INTRODUCTION

Every group of plants that is widely cultivated has generated many books on methods of cultivation and on the different forms, varieties or cultivars that are or could be made available for growing.

Roses, cacti and succulents, dahlias, chrysanthemums, houseplants and even vegetables and fruit have a vast literature on these aspects but orchids, despite their popularity, have not engendered this type of book very often. Even if nominally covering all aspects of orchids, with such subtitles as 'botany and culture', they have usually been written by somebody who is a real specialist in only one of these fields. Errors of fact, errors of omission, generalizations are a little too frequent. This book, written by an eminent orchid grower in a country where not only greenhouse orchid-culture is practised but also 'indoor' growing is more widespread than anywhere else and then translated and edited by a botanist and orchid systematist, will, we hope, redress the balance to a large extent.

There are many books on orchid culture but few enter into such detail as the present volume on, for example, the techniques of seed sowing, hybridization and meristem culture. The text has been revised only in so far as the latest discoveries or the special conditions and practices pertaining in the British Isles and North America have rendered it necessary.

The reader should stop at this point and only return to this introduction when the general text of the book has been fully read and explored...

By now even the keenest enthusiast may be wondering where he should proceed to maintain his interest in orchids, for even a well-stocked greenhouse palls after a while.

One appendix to this book (page 208) lists many other books on orchids and these themselves list many more books and articles: all are well worth reading. Many of the techniques may well be applied to your own collection or at least the scientific basis behind what you already do will be made clearer. Another appendix mentions the major orchid periodicals, some in English, some not, but all intended to keep you abreast of the latest developments in orchid culture and breeding as well as of the achievements of orchid 'personalities'.

On page 203 are listed the local orchid societies of Great Britain and the major national societies outside that country. All welcome members, most issue newsletters, bulletins or even glossy magazines and it is in your own interests to join one or more. If your local society is really active it is probably best to join that: friends will be made, plants exchanged and, perhaps most important, cultural information exchanged. Most local orchid societies are affiliated to a national society and many national societies, or at least prominent members of them, are elected to the world-wide International Orchid Commission on Classification, Nomenclature and Registration. This body exists, as its name suggests, to rationalize and sanction, internationally, procedures for the classification, nomenclature and registration of orchid hybrids. It does not, of course, interfere with botanical, taxonomic decisions, but does help by advising the Registrar of Orchid Hybrids, at the Royal Horticultural Society in London, on what names to adopt, for example. The first concrete example of the work of the IOCCNR is the *Handbook* (see pages 152 and 206).

If you do not become involved in the administration of an orchid society how else can you maintain and further your interest? Perhaps you feel like exhibiting some of your best blooms or finest grown plants at one of the monthly shows of your orchid society. Provided you have plants and flowers of reasonable quality this is not difficult; by observing the technique used by senior exhibitors you will learn exactly what type of plant to show, how to dress the pot with moss, how to stake the plants and how to pack it so that it travels unharmed. You will also learn how to 'hold back' flowers for a show some time ahead or how to ensure that all are out at the same time and the lower ones not setting large capsules. You may not have any really spectacular plants to show as individual exhibits but perhaps a group of about six plants would be possible. Beforehand try to find out what method of judging is used, whether the points-system or the visual appreciation. Eventually you may even enter plants before the Orchid Committee of the Royal Horticultural Society and gain an Award of Merit or Certificate of Cultural Commendation. The peak of an amateur enthusiast's ambition would be to stage a gold medal exhibit at an important flower show. This is possible, but it is more likely that you will be asked to contribute some plants for a joint amateur exhibit and you may well indeed thus be an important contributor towards a gold medal.

If you are not interested in joining a society, you may wish to start your own hybridization programme. Some of the most spectacular advances in orchid breeding have been made by the amateur working in a small greenhouse, diligently and patiently, until a champion cultivar of a new grex is produced. Another possible activity, though one which many amateurs find rather 'sordid' is the selling of seedlings or cut-flowers. This is certainly performing a most useful service to other growers and the cash obtained will enable you to improve your collection, build another greenhouse or update the present heating, ventilating or shading equipment.

Photographing or painting your orchid flowers, as well as being satisfying personally, often leads to commissions and publishers are always searching for illustrations for books and magazines.

To end on rather a sombre note... Do make certain before you are too old that you make your will and that your orchid collection is given pride of place in it. Your house, or your bank deposit will not deteriorate much in a short time on your death, but your orchid collection, so painstakingly accumulated over the years, will suffer irreparable damage if you are not there. Make sure that provision is made for its immediate care and, if it has to be disbanded, that it will be disposed of at the best prices. It may well be the most valuable part of your estate.

Such is the appeal of orchids that you never in your lifetime realize their financial value, but the contentment and relaxation they afford are beyond all such value.

E. Launert.
P. F. Hunt.

WHAT ORCHIDS ARE

For a full understanding of this book a certain amount of botanical knowledge is necessary. Orchids are members of the Orchidaceae, a family in the monocotyledons which are a major group of the Angiosperms or flowering plants.

At the present state of our knowledge the orchid family comprises about 17,000 species distributed among 750 genera.

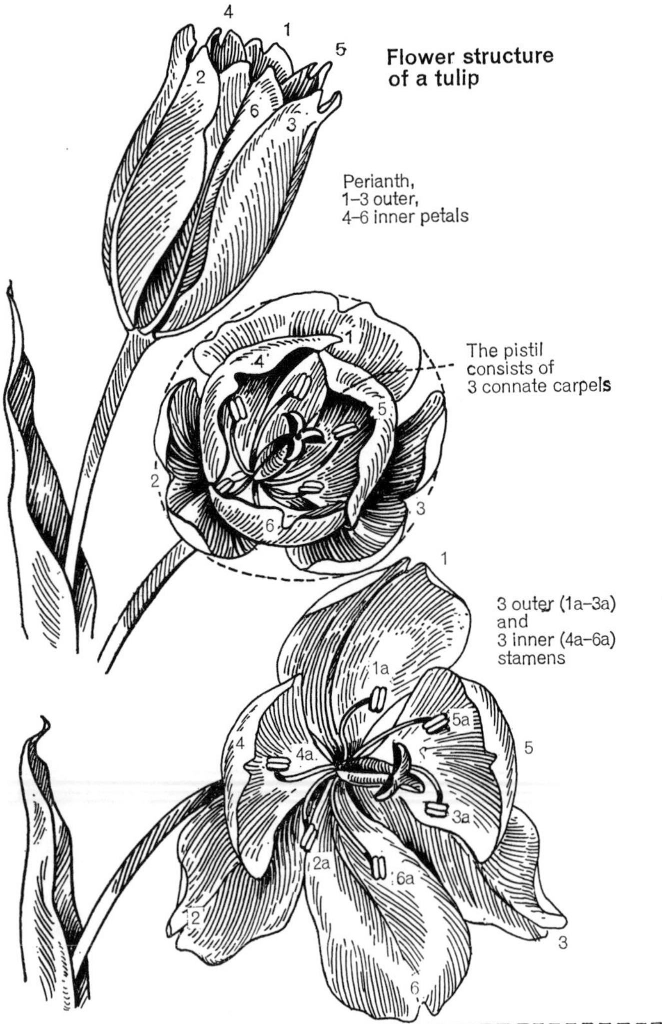

Flower structure of a tulip

Perianth,
1–3 outer,
4–6 inner petals

The pistil
consists of
3 connate carpels

3 outer (1a–3a)
and
3 inner (4a–6a)
stamens

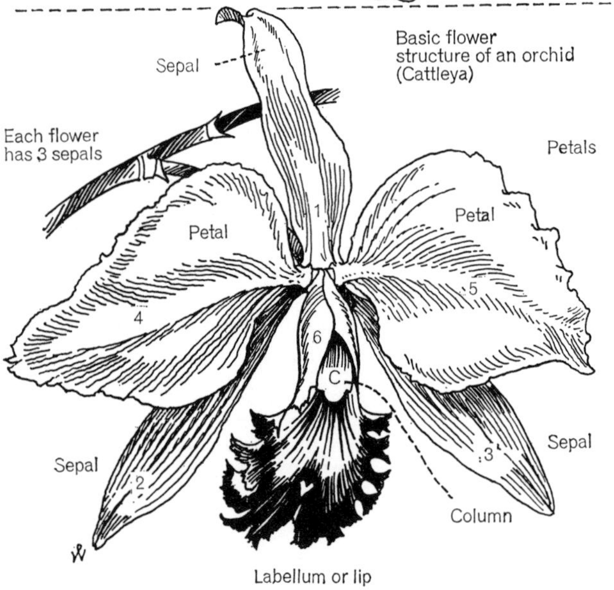

Sepal

Each flower
has 3 sepals

Basic flower
structure of an orchid
(Cattleya)

Petals

Petal

Petal

Sepal

Sepal

Sepal

Column

Labellum or lip

The flowers

In order to understand the structure of an orchid flower it is useful to compare it with another monocotyledonous flower such as a tulip. The sexual organs are enclosed, in the tulip, by a perianth composed of three outer sepals and three inner petals and consist of the stamens arranged in two whorls of three and the ovary composed of three carpels.

In the orchid flower this basic scheme is rearranged in a unique way. The three outer sepals are usually different in shape, as well as in colour, from the inner petals. Of the petals the two lateral ones are similar whereas the third usually differs considerably in size, shape, colour and ornamentation and is called the labellum, or lip. In Cattleya, for example, the labellum differs conspicuously in many ways but in some genera it is very inconspicuous being much smaller than the petals. Far more varied are the sexual organs! Out of the six stamens usually only one is fully developed and functional and this is united with the styles to form a single organ called the column. At the top of the column the anther is situated and is separated by a sterile lobe, the rostellum, from the stigma beneath.

In the subfamily Cypripedioideae, the Ladies' Slippers, a further

12

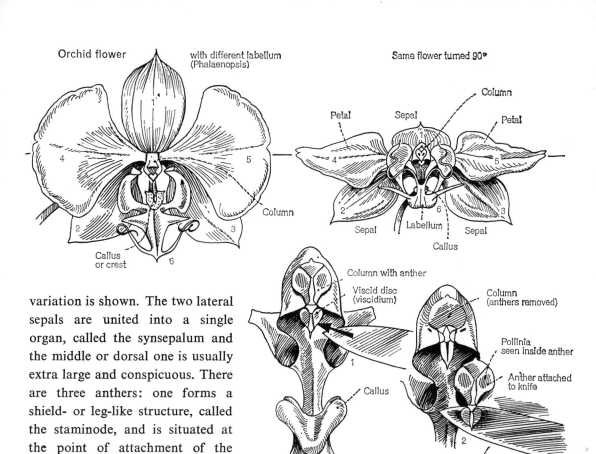

Orchid flower with different labellum (Phalaenopsis)

Same flower turned 90°

1

4 · 5

2 · 3

Column

Callus or crest · 6

Petal · Sepal · Column

4 · 5

2 · 6 · 3

Sepal · Labellum · Sepal

Callus

Column with anther

Viscid disc (viscidium)

Column (anthers removed)

Pollinia seen inside anther

Anther attached to knife

1

Callus

2

Anther viewed from beneath

Pollinia

4

Viscidium

3

Stipes

Insect leaving flower with pollinia attached to its body

Visiting insect aiming at callus

Natural pollination

variation is shown. The two lateral sepals are united into a single organ, called the synsepalum and the middle or dorsal one is usually extra large and conspicuous. There are three anthers: one forms a shield- or leg-like structure, called the staminode, and is situated at the point of attachment of the slipper-shaped labellum, and the other two are fertile and situated on either side of the short column just below the staminode.

The column in the subfamily Orchidoideae, to which 99 per cent of the species belong, is very varied in shape, size, colour and ornamentation. While most orchids are insect pollinated, a considerable number are fertilized by other creatures such as bats, snails and small birds, like humming-birds and bee-eaters, and a few are self-pollinated. One of the most striking differences between the orchids and other families is the vast number of seeds produced in each capsule.

13

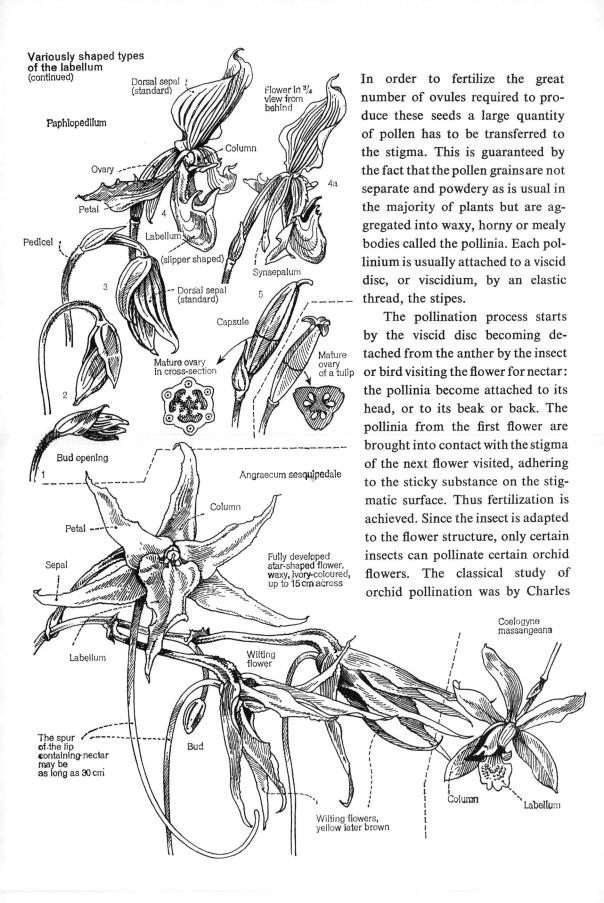

Variously shaped types of the labellum (continued)

Paphiopedilum

Dorsal sepal (standard)

Flower in ¾ view from behind

Column

4a

Ovary

Petal

4

Labellum

(slipper shaped)

Synsepalum

Pedicel

3

Dorsal sepal (standard)

5

Capsule

Mature ovary in cross-section

Mature ovary of a tulip

2

Bud opening

1

Angraecum sesquipedale

Column

Petal

Sepal

Fully developed star-shaped flower, waxy, ivory-coloured, up to 15 cm across

Coelogyne massangeana

Labellum

Wilting flower

The spur of the lip containing nectar may be as long as 30 cm

Bud

Wilting flowers, yellow later brown

Column

Labellum

In order to fertilize the great number of ovules required to produce these seeds a large quantity of pollen has to be transferred to the stigma. This is guaranteed by the fact that the pollen grains are not separate and powdery as is usual in the majority of plants but are aggregated into waxy, horny or mealy bodies called the pollinia. Each pollinium is usually attached to a viscid disc, or viscidium, by an elastic thread, the stipes.

The pollination process starts by the viscid disc becoming detached from the anther by the insect or bird visiting the flower for nectar: the pollinia become attached to its head, or to its beak or back. The pollinia from the first flower are brought into contact with the stigma of the next flower visited, adhering to the sticky substance on the stigmatic surface. Thus fertilization is achieved. Since the insect is adapted to the flower structure, only certain insects can pollinate certain orchid flowers. The classical study of orchid pollination was by Charles

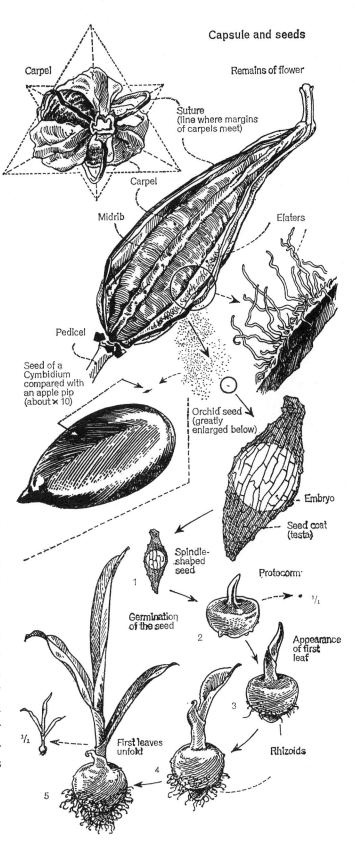

Darwin but the most comprehensive recent book on the subject is by Van der Pijl and Dodson (see p. 208).

Insects are attracted to the flowers by various devices. Besides nectar a variety of edible tissues are offered. Moreover intense scents and brilliant colours are frequently present. For example, in most Oncidium species, the large brilliant yellow labellum acts as a landing platform. Almost every orchid flower has at least one attractive device for ensuring pollination and the consequent survival of the species. One often wonders why the orchids have developed such complex adaptations to ensure their pollination when most other flowers survive on far simpler structures!

In the opening orchid flower the ovary, situated just below the sepals at the top of each individual stem or pedicel, is small and inconspicuous, but after pollination it enlarges considerably as the pollen-tubes grow slowly down from the stigma into the ovules. Although the petals and sepals start to wilt and wither only a short time after pollination the actual fertilization of the ovules takes place perhaps weeks or even months later. Even after this often considerable delay the seed of most orchids takes a further long period to mature: for example, Dendrobium and Phalaenopsis take about 4 months

15

Carpel

Carpel

Midrib

Pedicel

Remains of flower

Suture
(line where margins
of carpels meet)

Elaters

Seed of a
Cymbidium
compared with
an apple pip
(about × 10)

Orchid seed
(greatly
enlarged below)

Embryo

Seed coat
(testa)

Spindle-
shaped
seed

1

Germination
of the seed

Protocorm

2

$^1/_1$

Appearance
of first
leaf

3

$^1/_1$

First leaves
unfold

Rhizoids

4

5

altogether, Cattleya and Paphiopedilum 10–12 months and Vanda, 15 months! Orchids native to temperate regions, however, usually take a much shorter time for their seed capsules to mature.

It is interesting to realize that despite the extraordinary variation in their flowers the seed capsules of orchids are relatively uniform. They are 3-locular, globose or spindle-shaped and bear longitudinal ridges or channels.

Green at first, the capsules turn yellow and finally brown when they dehisce as three or six longitudinal slits appear. These remain partially connected by fibres and the seeds are dispersed slowly, often over several days, through the mesh formed by these fibres. In the interior of the capsule there are elaters, or paraphyses which, reacting hygroscopically with the atmospheric humidity, further regulate seed dispersal.

Orchid seeds are by far the smallest in the flowering plant kingdom but to compensate for this they are produced in vast quantities. For example, in *Dactylorhiza maculata* each capsule contains about 6200 seeds, Cymbidium has 1,500,000, Maxillaria about 1,700,000 and Cattleya up to 5 million. Since a plant usually bears more than one fruit an inconceivable number of seeds is produced by each plant.

The seeds are devoid of any food reserves, containing little other than the minute embryo surrounded by a net-like seed coat; consequently they are very light, each weighing no more than a few millionths of a gram. It is possible that the seed coat functions as a steering device for the air-borne dispersed seeds and it possibly has a further use during germination. In contrast with the seed of many other plants the viability of an orchid seed is relatively short, not more than six months under normal, natural conditions, although modern methods have been developed to extend this. The almost weightless nature of the seeds is connected with their dispersal: they drift downwards slowly, spreading widely and thus the chances of a seed eventually landing on a spot favourable for germination are increased. Often wind currents will carry them upwards to great heights and for considerable distances laterally.

Because of the absence of a food supply in the seeds they cannot successfully germinate and grow independently. They rely on a symbiotic relationship with a mycorrhizal fungus, the hyphae of which have to be present in the soil. The germinating seedlings' first nutriment is supplied by the fungus which soon enters most parts of the developing plant, remaining there throughout the orchid's life. This symbiosis was first discovered by the French botanist Noel Bernard who published his findings in 1904.

The time taken for seeds to germinate varies greatly both with the species involved and with the period the seeds have taken to ripen. With the majority of species, in about a month the cylinder-shaped embryos develop into top-shaped structures which, by their greenish colour, exhibit the first stages of chlorophyll

Eria pannea

1 Pleione humilis; 2 Pleione hookerana; 3 Dendrobium gibsonii; 4 Dendrobium devonianum;
5 Pleurothallis species; 6 Kefersteinia mystacina

development, accompanied by the production of very fine root-hair-like rhizoids. A few weeks later the first leaves develop and these are followed by true roots. Over the next few years the development of the plant continues. We do not know how long it takes under natural conditions for most tropical orchids to reach the flowering state from germination but it can vary up to many years depending on the species and the immediate environment of the individual plant.

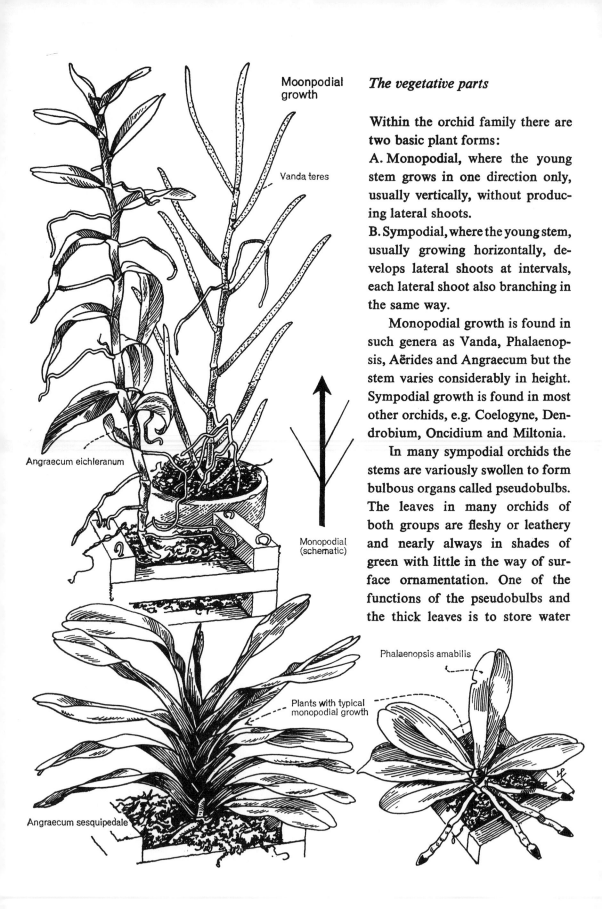

Moonpodial growth

Vanda teres

Angraecum eichleranum

Monopodial
(schematic)

Angraecum sesquipedale

Plants with typical
monopodial growth

Phalaenopsis amabilis

The vegetative parts

Within the orchid family there are two basic plant forms:

A. Monopodial, where the young stem grows in one direction only, usually vertically, without producing lateral shoots.

B. Sympodial, where the young stem, usually growing horizontally, develops lateral shoots at intervals, each lateral shoot also branching in the same way.

Monopodial growth is found in such genera as Vanda, Phalaenopsis, Aërides and Angraecum but the stem varies considerably in height. Sympodial growth is found in most other orchids, e.g. Coelogyne, Dendrobium, Oncidium and Miltonia.

In many sympodial orchids the stems are variously swollen to form bulbous organs called pseudobulbs. The leaves in many orchids of both groups are fleshy or leathery and nearly always in shades of green with little in the way of surface ornamentation. One of the functions of the pseudobulbs and the thick leaves is to store water and nutrients during periods when these are not readily available from the plants' environment.

The inflorescences of monopodial orchids are always borne laterally but the sympodials can have both lateral and terminal flower spikes.

The roots

As well as serving as water and food obtaining organs, the roots of epiphytic orchids have the prime function of anchoring the plants in their lofty aerial positions towards the tops of jungle trees. These roots can either be closely adherent to the bark of the host tree, or, in some cases, rock surface or may merely be suspended in the air. Although usually cylindrical, aerial roots can also be ribbon-like as in Phalaenopis. They contain some chlorophyll and thereby assimilate food by photosynthesis or, in extreme cases, as with Microcoelia and Taeniophyllum, the plants never bear leaves at all, the entire food production being carried on by the roots. In some orchids photosynthesis is carried out by the flowers themselves which are green in colour!

Generally the roots of epiphytes are surrounded by layers of dead silverish-grey empty cells, called the velamen, and only the growing root tip is green. The velamen is able to absorb moisture from the air and thus insulate the

21

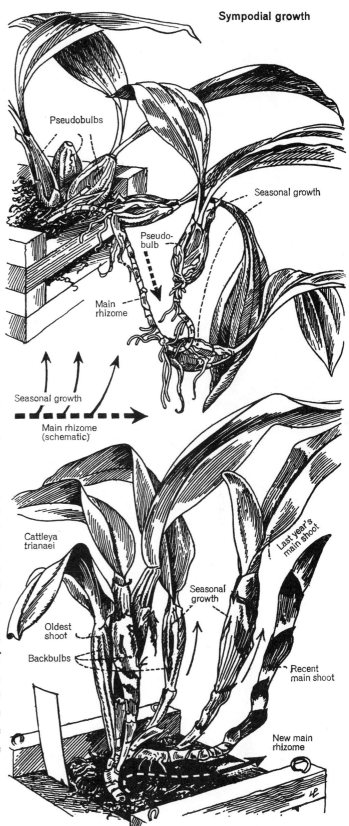

Pseudobulbs

Seasonal growth

Pseudo-bulb

Main rhizome

Seasonal growth

Main rhizome
(schematic)

Cattleya
trianaei

Last year's
main shoot

Seasonal
growth

Oldest
shoot

Backbulbs

Recent
main shoot

New main
rhizome

Inflorescenses (flower spikes) of sympodial orchids

Pseudo-bulb

Terminal inflorescence

Cattleya trianaei

Lateral flower-spike (developing)

Coelogyne massangeana

Pseudobulb

Gongora galeata

Pseudobulb

Inflorescence

Developing inflorescence

Inflorescence with buds

Unopened bud

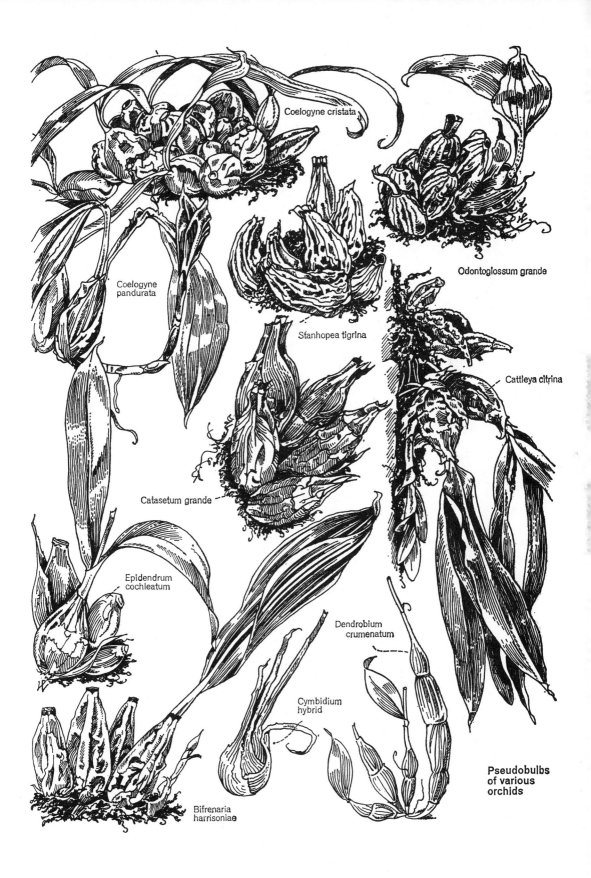

Coelogyne cristata

Odontoglossum grande

Coelogyne pandurata

Stanhopea tigrina

Cattleya citrina

Catasetum grande

Epidendrum cochleatum

Dendrobium crumenatum

Cymbidium hybrid

Pseudobulbs of various orchids

Bifrenaria harrisoniae

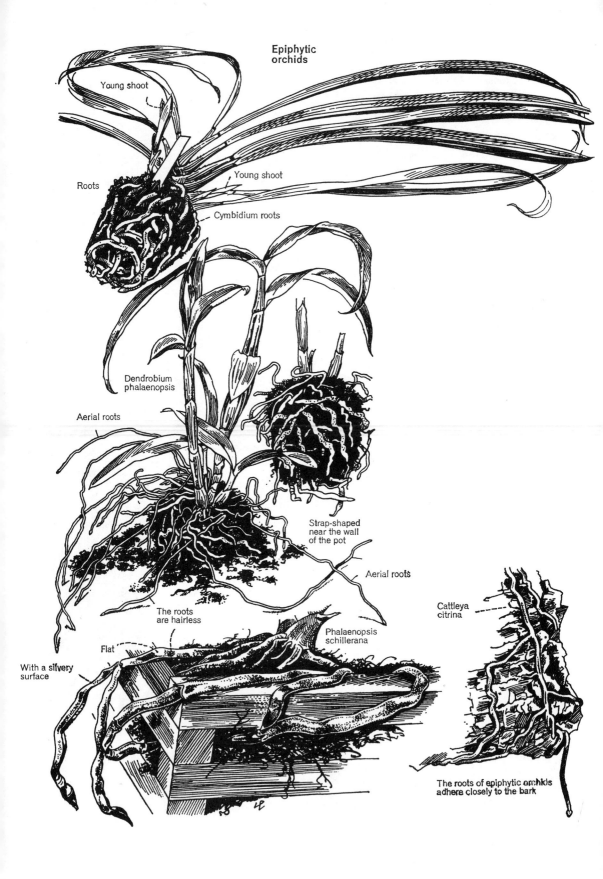

Epiphytic
orchids

Young shoot

Young shoot

Roots

Cymbidium roots

Dendrobium
phalaenopsis

Aerial roots

Strap-shaped
near the wall
of the pot

Aerial roots

The roots
are hairless

Flat

Phalaenopsis
schillerana

Cattleya
citrina

With a silvery
surface

The roots of epiphytic orchids
adhere closely to the bark

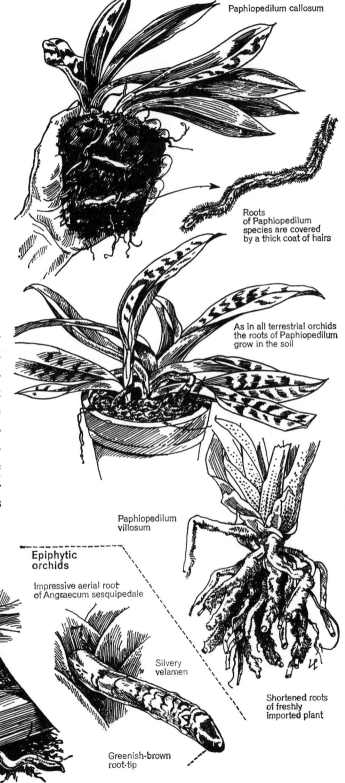

Paphiopedilum callosum

Roots of Paphiopedilum species are covered by a thick coat of hairs

As in all terrestrial orchids the roots of Paphiopedilum grow in the soil

Paphiopedilum villosum

Shortened roots of freshly imported plant

root from excessive temperatures. It does not pass water into the root itself, this function being carried out only by the unclothed root tip. Damage to this root tip is detrimental to the well-being of the plant.

Terrestrial orchids, such as Paphiopedilum, have relatively few but strongly developed roots covered by a thick pelt of root hairs, the root tip again being the only uncovered part.

Other terrestrial orchids, such as our native temperate species, develop more ordinary roots. Many of these native orchids are not winter-green because of considerable climatic vagaries, but their survival is guaranteed by the production of tubers and thick rhizomes. The aerial parts of the plant die down at the approach of the unfavourable season but the subterranean organs can remain dormant for several years. They are globular, ellipsoid, digitate or testiculate, do not develop many roots and are easily injured.

Aerial roots

Phalaenopsis amabilis

Epiphytic orchids

Impressive aerial root of Angraecum sesquipedale

Silvery velamen

Greenish-brown root-tip

DISTRIBUTION

The orchid family is the largest in the plant kingdom and is distributed throughout the world, although certain areas have more than others. Some genera are world-wide in their distribution or at least pan-tropical, but others are much more limited. However, there are two main centres: the Old World and the New World tropics. About 80 per cent of the known species occur in these two areas, with only 20 per cent in the temperate zones. Less than 1 per cent of the world's orchids are native to Europe and less than 1.5 per cent are found in North America. New Guinea and Borneo, however, probably contain 20 per cent of the total species so far known.

In the cooler areas, and in the even colder subarctic zone, all species are terrestrial herbaceous perennials showing marked seasonal adaptations. The tropical orchids, however, are largely epiphytic, i.e. they live on trees or rocks although they do not obtain their food parasitically from them. The climate basically determines the presence of ephipytes. Their distribution depends to a certain extent on temperature but is largely governed by atmospheric humidity and precipitation. Most epiphytes are found in areas of high rainfall distributed more or less evenly throughout the year: these conditions pertain in the area between the Tropics of Cancer and Capricorn, i.e. about 23°N and S of the Equator. As far as the land mass in this tropical belt is concerned about half consists of very dry country and here orchids are only rarely found. The epiphytes are concentrated in the rainy areas to the seaward sides of mountain ranges. These areas are the rain forests or true jungles where moisture is always present. Even up to 4200 m altitude, in the Andes of Peru and Colombia, many epiphytic orchids occur and even survive regular frosts. Likewise in Asia, for example in the Himalayas, epiphytic orchids are found up to 2600 m.

The well-known *Coelogyne cristata* ranges from 2000 to 2400 m. The probable reason why the altitudinal range is not quite so high in such areas as the Himalayas when compared with the Andes is the closer proximity to the sea of the latter region.

Although many species are confined to a relatively limited area and are termed 'endemics' others are very widely distributed. To generalize: the orchids of the north temperate regions tend to be more widely distributed than their tropical congeners. One of the most beautiful temperate orchids, *Cypripedium calceolus*, ranges from north America to Britain and across Europe into Siberia. *Cypripedium guttatum*, although not occuring in Europe proper, is found from the USSR through Alaska to British Columbia. Nevertheless a few tropical species, such as the well-known *Cirrhopetalum umbellatum*, have been found from Africa through Madagascar and the Mascarenes to Borneo, New Guinea, northern Australia and so on, to Fiji and Tahiti.

Again, as a generalization, most of the better known genera are confined to a

Epiphytes

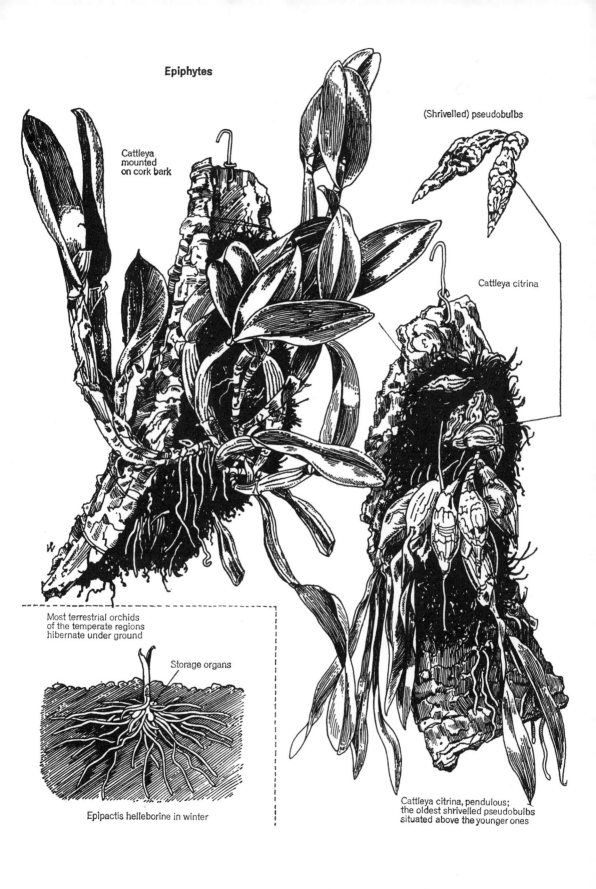

Cattleya
mounted
on cork bark

(Shrivelled) pseudobulbs

Cattleya citrina

Most terrestrial orchids
of the temperate regions
hibernate under ground

Storage organs

Epipactis helleborine in winter

Cattleya citrina, pendulous;
the oldest shrivelled pseudobulbs
situated above the younger ones

Storage organs of terrestrial orchids

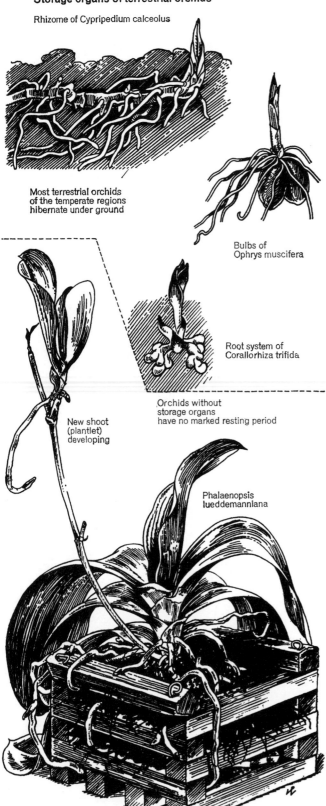

Rhizome of Cypripedium calceolus

Most terrestrial orchids
of the temperate regions
hibernate under ground

Bulbs of
Ophrys muscifera

Root system of
Corallorhiza trifida

Orchids without
storage organs
have no marked resting period

New shoot
(plantlet)
developing

Phalaenopsis
lueddemanniana

single continent, or at least to a well-defined area. Examples are Coelogyne, Dendrobium, Paphiopedilum, Vanda and Phalaenopsis confined to tropical Asia, with occasionally a few species in Australia; tropical American endemic genera include Cattleya, Laelia, Lycaste, Masdevallia, Oncidium and Odontoglossum.

Interestingly both Africa and Australia are relatively poor in native orchids of great horticultural merit. Nevertheless their small flowered species, often in dull colours, have a certain charm and such 'botanicals' are often collected and grown by enthusiasts. Madagascar, again, is poor in showy species, with the exception of a few plants such as *Angraecum sesquipedale, Cymbidiella rhodocheila* and certain Gastrorchis species but makes up for this by a fantastic wealth of botanicals and miniatures.

The key to the successful cultivation of orchids is a knowledge of their native haunts. Especially important is a knowledge of the microclimate in which each species grows. Unfortunately we still know very little about the natural origin of many of the orchids we grow: knowing the name of the country of origin is of little use unless more exact data are also available.

28

ECOLOGY

Very little is known about the ecology of orchids but the conditions under which epiphytes and terrestrials grow are certainly vastly different. Terrestrial orchids behave basically in the same way as any other terrestrial plant, being subject to such factors as soil acidity and competition for light and water. Species of the tropical genus, Sobralia, grow in great masses and very closely resemble the common reed, Phragmites, growing in marshes and estuaries. Epiphytes can be found on all kinds of 'host' trees but tend to prefer certain species probably because of the texture of their bark. Many are found at the lowest levels of the trees, towards the bases of their trunks, whereas others occupy the tips of the highest branches. The latter are very highly adapted to their very hot, sunny and frequently very dry perches, often having terete or thick, fleshy leaves. Some epiphytes grow on precipitous rock, e.g. *Cattleya percivaliana, Dendrobium speciosum* and *Coelogyne cristata*. To grow these, and many of the more normal epiphytes, they should be kept in the intertwining felt of roots and humus which they have produced.

Although in the tropical belt, orchids are not subject to significant differences in the relative lengths of day and night at different times of

Many orchids have their storage organs above ground

Odontoglossum grande

Pseudobulbs

Some orchids shed their leaves after the annual shoot has matured (e.g. Catasetum)

Leaves of annual shoot not yet shed

Older pseudobulbs without their leaves

Catasetum scurra

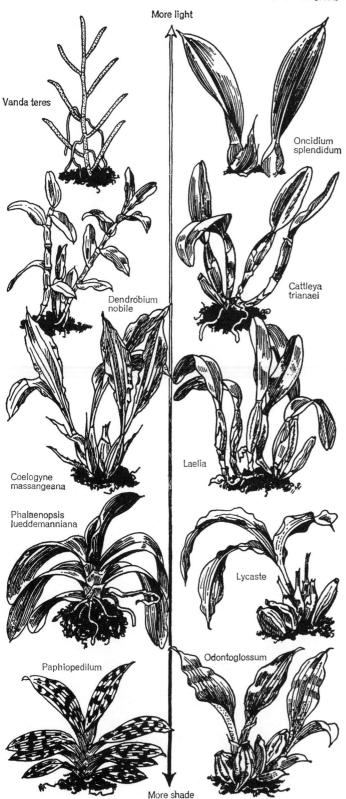

Orchids originating
in South East Asia

Orchids originating
in South and Central America

More light

Vanda teres

Oncidium
splendidum

Dendrobium
nobile

Cattleya
trianaei

Coelogyne
massangeana

Laelia

Phalaenopsis
lueddemanniana

Lycaste

Paphiopedilum

Odontoglossum

More shade

the year, and temperatures also vary but little from one month to the next, there can be seasonal changes in rainfall. In fact we can roughly divide tropical orchids into those that grow in areas where there are these seasonal differences and those that experience no consistent changes at all in any year. Examples would be the deciduous Dendrobiums that occur in the Himalayas and which require a well marked dry resting period and the evergreen New Guinea Dendrobium species in which the culture must remain constant from month to month.

It may be useful to give the following scheme for the vegetative classification of epiphytes in relation to their cultivation requirements

1 Fleshy leaves, no pseudobulbs, evergreen. No direct sunlight, plenty of shade, and no resting period. Example: *Phalaenopsis amabilis.*

2 Thin leaves, strongly developed pseudobulbs, deciduous (at end of growing period). Semi-shade, plenty of moisture during growing period but withhold water entirely during resting period. Example: *Catasetum scurra.*

3 Leathery leaves, usually well developed pseudobulbs, evergreen or deciduous. Semi-shade usually but more light for good pseudobulb development, plenty of mois-

30

Light

Leaves gradually become broader and softer

Shade

Tough leaf

Leaf-lamina absent

Large soft green leaf-lamina

There is a correlation between leaf-structure and light requirement

Plants adapted to light

Oncidium splendidum

Vanda teres

Bifrenaria harrisoniae

Semi-shade

Paphiopedilum

Plants adapted to shady habitats

Phalaenopsis amabilis

31

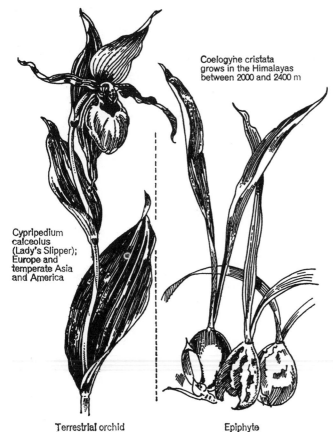

Coelogyne cristata
grows in the Himalayas
between 2000 and 2400 m

Cypripedium
calceolus
(Lady's Slipper);
Europe and
temperate Asia
and America

Terrestrial orchid

Epiphyte

ture during growing period but moderate amounts (sufficient to avoid shrinkage of pseudobulbs) during resting period. Example: *Cattleya trianaei.*

4 Leathery leaves, no pseudobulbs. Plenty of light, plenty of moisture during growing period but moderate amounts only during resting period. Example: *Oncidium splendidum.*

5 Terete and semi-terete leaves, no pseudobulbs. Very strong light, plenty of moisture during growing period, moderate amount during resting period. Example: *Vanda teres.*

Unfortunately this scheme does not give any indication of the correct temperatures required: this has to be gained from knowledge of the species' 'habitats'.

CHOOSING ORCHIDS

People grow orchids for various reasons. The most important, perhaps, is their aesthetic appeal but there is also the mystery which surrounds them, as well, of course, as their commercial value.

Recently the hobby of orchid growing has gained many new converts and generally higher standards of living have contributed to this trend. With modern advances in technology it is becoming increasingly easier to grow orchids successfully although even today many aspects of culture are in their infancy. One of the most striking developments is the provision of correct lighting conditions by artificial means. While light is probably the most important factor influencing plant growth, heat is also very important and by modern methods of electrical heating it is possible to control carefully the temperatures of greenhouses and indoor mini-greenhouses. Even the problem of keeping the humidity at the required level is no longer serious.

This book is intended as a guide for all those orchid-lovers who already grow or would like to grow their favourite flowers. Though it caters mainly for the beginner, the more advanced grower and those who have already succeeded in cultivating orchids will find it contains some useful hints. The absolute beginner may be daunted by the formidable list of essential requirements for successful cultivation but it would be irresponsible not to point out the care that is necessary to, more or less, reach perfection. Undoubtedly, the care of orchids is far more difficult and exacting than that of other plants, and the gardener who succeeds in orchid growing can look on it as the crowning success of his horticultural career.

The beginner will perhaps first wish to grow those orchids whose beauty has struck him at a flower show, in a florist's shop, in a botanical garden or even in books and advertisements.

One point must be made clear at once: it is impossible to grow orchids from different climatic conditions in the same place since their temperature requirements can be so different. They have to be cultivated in separate places. How is this to be achieved?

33

Quite handsome –
but only suited to the greenhouse

Too large for the plant window!

Angraecum sesquipedale

Height (incl. basket) 85 cm
width 72 cm

Aeriál roots

Monopodial growth

The various conditions pertaining in the wild have already been discussed in general terms (p. 29), but for cultivation we recognize only three temperature régimes, cool, intermediate and warm. If the grower knows the climatic conditions from which his favourite plants came he can decide which of these three temperature régimes best suits them.

34

1 Dendrobium phalaenopsis; 2 Phaphiopendilum; 3 Cattleya; 4 Cycnoches

1 Oncidium 'Anne Warne' × Rodriguezia decora; 2 Odontoglossum rossii; 3 Phalaenopsis schillerana

In the older literature only relatively few species are mentioned as being capable of cultivation but this point of view has now changed. With careful attention and a 'feeling' for plants much can be achieved. In the small indoor greenhouses mentioned earlier modern control equipment enables one to grow a surprisingly wide range of species. However, if you wish to grow orchids indoors, merely as house plants (and not in these special containers), the choice is necessarily limited to those that require the same environmental conditions as yourself!

Of obvious importance too is the size of the plants in relation to the amount of space available. After a time plants of most Dendrobiums, Cattleyas, Vandas and Cymbidiums

Young plants
are difficult to begin with

Cattleya
which has not
yet flowered

Recommended
stage

Cattleya
(young plants)

4 years old

Only for the really
experienced amateur

3 years old

Orchid-kindergarten
(only for the
advanced amateur)

Even smaller plants
(these should be left
to the specialist)

Young specimens
of Paphiopedilum,
2½-years old

2 years old

Young specimen
of Cattleya

This plant has
also not yet flowered

The plant should be acquired
at this stage

37

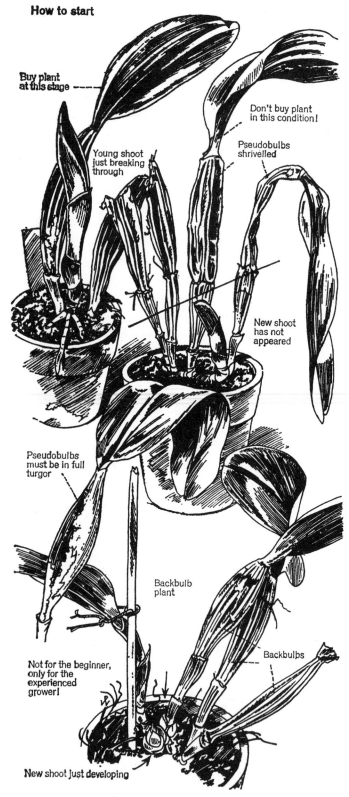

Buy plant
at this stage

Don't buy plant
in this condition!

Young shoot
just breaking
through

Pseudobulbs
shrivelled

New shoot
has not
appeared

Pseudobulbs
must be in full
turgor

Backbulb
plant

Backbulbs

Not for the beginner,
only for the
experienced
grower!

New shoot just developing

New plants can be derived from backbulbs

become too large for the average indoor greenhouse. Though this does not only apply to orchids! Even small plants may develop such long and heavy flower spikes that difficulties may arise. Nonetheless, by careful selection, a relatively large yet varied collection can be housed in a fairly small space. If space is very limited one or two larger orchids can be accompanied by several miniatures or 'botanicals'. The care of the latter, however, often needs 'green fingers' or at least a careful prior study of their light, air and humidity requirements. Many thrive on bark.

Of course it is quite understandable that the enthusiast wishes to have his plants flower at certain seasons, especially in the late autumn, winter and early spring, but the flowering times of the plants he especially admires do not always allow this. At these times also, conditions in the home are not always conducive to flowering. Without additional lighting Cattleya flowers quickly wilt and fade or may even not open at all. Even during the summer months conditions may not be quite right! Probably early spring and early autumn are the best times for orchid growing in the home. Certain orchids have varying flowering times and much can be achieved by compromise. Nevertheless casualties can and do occur, but not frequently.

38

The tyro often thinks that a plant given to him in flower at a particular time will come into bloom again at the same time the next year but environmental conditions often render this assumption quite incorrect. If you especially desire a particular orchid to be in flower at a particular time the only advice that can be offered is to grow as many plants of the species or hybrid as possible: their inherent variability will often give the desired result. If you would like to have an orchid in flower at all times of the year it is not necessarily advisable to buy, say, a dozen different plants each with a different flowering period: you actually need several plants of the twelve different species or hybrids chosen. However, by slowly building up your collection by propagation, over the years, you may finally achieve your ideal.

The beginner may wish to select a flower colour scheme for certain times but this is too ambitious for all but the owner of a very large and varied collection. However, again compensating for this hard fact, named orchid species and cultivars of hybrid grexes are remarkably constant in their flower colours. A red-flowered Cattleya species or hybrid will always be red-flowered. On the other hand if unflowered seedlings of hybrid grexes are purchased there is no guarantee of a particular flower colour. The result of crossing two plants may give a remarkable range of flower colours in the hybrid plants produced. A named cultivar of such a grex however will always be constant.

The same applies to flower size: within a species the size of the petals, sepals and lip vary very little. For the commercial grower size is at least as important as colour and may even be the overriding criterion for a plant's success in the cut-flower trade. For the amateur, however, the smaller flowers are often more useful, especially since they tend to last longer than the over-grown, over-blown specimens found in florists' shops.

Flower shape too is constant within a given species or cultivar of a hybrid grex and again is an important commercial consideration. Today's international fashion is away from the proper 'orchid' shape, with well defined sepals and lip (fenestration), towards a very flat shape with no spaces between the floral members (non-fenestration).

Whatever plants a beginner wishes to grow, whether large or small, bright or pastel coloured, of usual or bizarre shaped flowers, he should always start off his collection by purchasing plants more or less of flowering size. The advanced grower will often buy smaller plants or even just established seedlings in order to obtain the exact plants he requires. In any case large specimens may not be available of rarities or if they are the price is prohibitive. With smaller plants a waiting period of two or even three or four years is inevitable before the plants finally come into flower.

The purchase of plants just coming into flower was recommended above, but.

Rare orchids,
although fascinating,
pose difficult problems
even for the specialist

Isochilus
linearis

Brassavola
flagellaris

even this can lead to disappointment. The flowers may not last long or may not even open, dropping off as buds instead. Even very rudimentary buds may suddenly stop developing. All this can and does happen but is by no means inevitable.

However, if a just purchased plant is placed in a greenhouse the chances of it failing to flower quickly are greatly reduced.

The best thing to do is to buy a plant just coming into growth or even in the resting phase: it will be much more adaptable to its new conditions. If the plant is at the right age it will certainly flower the same year. If, however, you, buy young plants in order to increase your collection you must be prepared to wait until they reach flowering age—but it is a great experience when they do flower!

A relatively cheap way of increasing your collection is by dividing your own plants (see p. 100), but here again patience is needed for the backbulbs to develop flowering size plants.

So far we have been discussing only naturally occurring species and have briefly referred to artificial hybrids, but, of course, there are also natural hybrids. These are rare, however, because, for a natural hybrid to be formed there have to be two closely related plants growing in reasonable proximity. Because they are pollinated by insects or other animals, or self pollinated, natural hybridization is only possible between plants which grow relatively close to each other and flower simultaneously. However, man has overcome these natural sterility barriers: as some pollinia can be stored, under special conditions, for a considerable time it is even possible to cross plants which have different flowering periods. The great importance of this man-induced hybridization is that the resulting hybrids can outshine both parents, and for the commercial grower this is a primary factor in attracting the buying public especially where cut-flowers are concerned.

For various reasons the orthodox botanist is not altogether fond of artificial hybrids but the average grower may wish to strike the balance between species and hybrids. However, the geneticist and grower alike get great thrills from altering nature and from testing the limits of a plant's variability. The belief that hybrids are not so vigorous as species has long been disproved: in fact they are often hardier and more floriferous than species.

Another way of building up your collection is by importing plants from their native country, though this certainly cannot be recommended for the beginner! It should be undertaken only by the professional grower and by the amateur of long experience. For plants taken directly from their native haunts, a long period of acclimatization is often necessary (p. 96). Years ago the majority of imported orchids died before they could be sold, but nowadays with speedy air transport this loss factor has been greatly diminished. Plants that have not travelled for too long are much easier to establish than those imported by slower means.

I shall now sum up the types of orchids best suited to different groups of growers:

The beginner: stout, flowering-size plants with simple requirements which do not need changes in temperature and light at different seasons.

The more advanced grower: younger, not necessarily fully-developed, plants with varying light and temperature requirements.

The expert: young plants not fully developed, backbulbs and imported plants. (He cannot really do without a well equipped greenhouse!)

41

The perfectionist: species with very exacting requirements, often grown from seed, and often from hybrids he has raised himself. (A large greenhouse with all the modern equipment and control devices is required!)

What really counts in the end is the sum total of your own experience! The various great successes and dismal failures any grower doubtless experiences are not always explicable. It is possible that many of the things I have said, and will say, will not hold good in your particular case – you may be successful with a difficult subject without really trying, though more often the opposite will be the case! For the beginner failures are inevitable; the more advanced grower will also certainly experience many; with the expert, failures are still possible and they are not wholly unknown even to the perfectionist. But do not despair, rather try to discover the reasons for your failures. You will probably find that not only is your treatment of the plants at fault but also your initial selection.

HOUSING YOUR PLANTS

The following section considers those places where plants may successfully be grown, from the simplest location to the most sophisticated greenhouse. Success, however, is not necessarily dependent on the amount and quality of the growing equipment but also on the skill and experience of the grower.

1 The window sill
2 The 'plantarium' or indoor 'mini-greenhouse'
3 The 'plant window'
4 The true greenhouse

We shall also consider a fifth possibility which may well commend itself to the owner of a large old house, the basement.

On the window sill

In a plantarium

In the living room

Light?

Fresh air?

Humidity?

Outside the house

Outside the living room

Heatable greenhouse

Plant window set apart from the room (own independent climate)

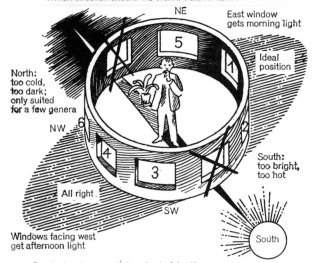

Which direction should the orchid window face?

NE

East window gets morning light

5

1

Ideal position

North: too cold, too dark; only suited for a few genera

NW 6

4

3

2

South: too bright, too hot

All right

SW

South

Windows facing west get afternoon light

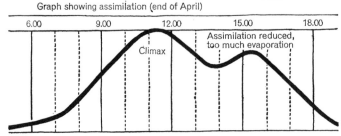

Graph showing assimilation (end of April)

| 6.00 | 9.00 | 12.00 | 15.00 | 18.00 |

Climax

Assimilation reduced, too much evaporation

Peak is reached before noon; during early afternoon often reduction caused by high temperatures

Growing plants on the window sill

The most important factor here is the position of the window. The most suitable are those facing east, south-east, south-west and west. For a southerly facing window some degree of shading will be necessary at the hottest times of the year. If there are no trees casting their shadows near the window some shade may be necessary at the other times as well. A well-designed canopy over the window reduces direct sunlight yet still gives ample light for good growth. Nowadays Venetian blinds are in fashion: they are either metallic or plastic and in both cases have glossy reflective surfaces. They are useful but since they occupy a considerable amount of window space their utility must be considered with some reservation. Exterior lamellated shutters are again coming into fashion but these or louvre windows are not ideal and should be used only as a last resort.

In order to house the plants comfortably the window sill may well have to be widened. During the cold season the plants should not be placed too near the glass or they may suffer frost damage. A damp atmosphere can be maintained around the plants by filling plastic, metal or earthenware trays with water in which are placed absorbent clay flower pots. The pots should be

44

1 Odontoglossum bictoniense; **2** Oncidium forbesii; **3** Catasetum pileatum; **4** Oncidium lanceanum

1 Eria barbarossa; 2 Dinema 'Epidendrum' polybalbon; 3 Cattleya intermedia; 4 Bifrenaria harrisoniae;
5 Laeliocattleya elegans; 6 Laeliocattleya Britannia ' Alba'; 7 Brassocattleya 'Daffodil';
8 Brassocattleya 'Toska'

1 Brassavola flagellaris; **2** Brassia verrucosa; **3** Phalaenopsis Grace Palm; **4** Phalaenopsis Monique; **5** Oncidium varicosum rogersii; **6** Dendrochilum glumaceum; **7** Odontoglossum crispum **8** Angevaecum eburneum

1 Dendrobium 'Anne-Marie'; 2 D. phalaenopsis 'Lady Fay'; 3 D. victoriae-reginae; 4 D. phalaenopsis var. compactum; 5 D. phalaenopsis 'American Beauty'; 6 D. nobile (left) D. Gatton Monarch (right)

touching one another as this dense arrangement creates as damp an atmosphere as possible over the entire surface. The usefulness of frequent spraying is debatable because the excessively dry atmosphere of the rest of the room will inevitably counteract this so quickly as to render the spraying noneffective. The only advantage in spraying is in keeping the potting compost evenly moist, but there is then the danger that it may become too damp and this can lead to root rot. Moreover spraying can have a deleterious effect on the window panes, window frames, the carpet and the furniture and may make the orchid enthusiast very unpopular with the rest of the household.

Since the plants grown on window sills are to a certain extent influenced by the general atmosphere of the room, usually the living room, the number of suitable species is limited.

Theoretically one would assume that orchids from areas of moderate humidity would find window sill conditions most favourable but these same species are also subject to a well-defined resting period which needs a relatively low temperature. Unfortunately this resting period coincides with the heating period in our living rooms when the day temperature averages around 20 °C (68 °F) but often with a marked

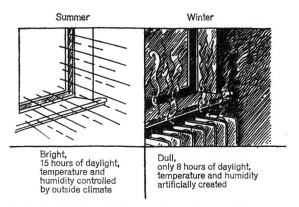

Summer	Winter
Bright, 15 hours of daylight, temperature and humidity controlled by outside climate	Dull, only 8 hours of daylight, temperature and humidity artificially created

Distribution of light in a first-floor room (percentage in relation to outside sunlight). Opposite the SE-window there is a grey building 20 m away; the NE-window faces an open space

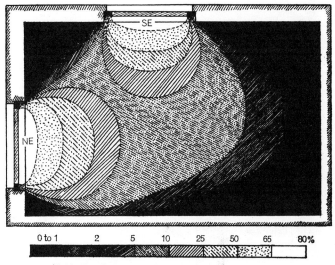

0 to 1   2   5   10   25   50   65   **80%**

Light intensity measured 1 m above floor
room dimensions 4.20×6.40 m; height of window sill 1.50 m; width of window 2 m

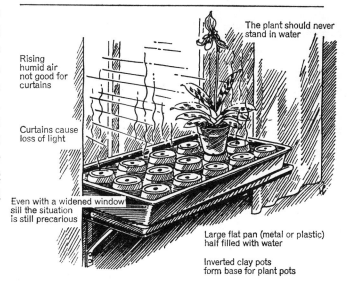

The plant should never stand in water

Rising humid air not good for curtains

Curtains cause loss of light

Even with a widened window sill the situation is still precarious

Large flat pan (metal or plastic) half filled with water

Inverted clay pots form base for plant pots

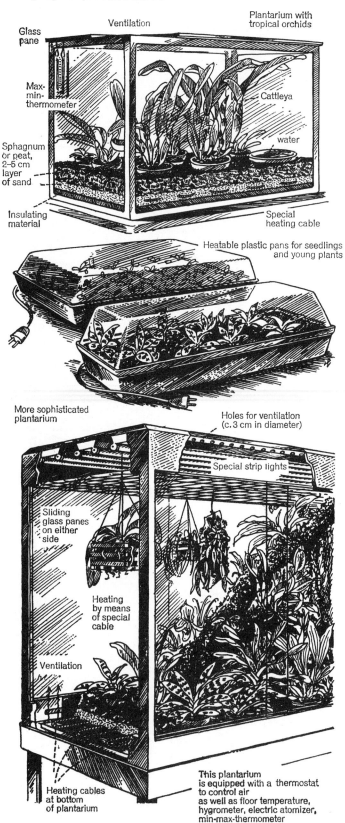

Simple plantarium
(plenty of scope for improvisation)

Glass pane

Ventilation

Plantarium with tropical orchids

Max-min-thermometer

Cattleya

water

Sphagnum or peat, 2–5 cm layer of sand

Insulating material

Special heating cable

Heatable plastic pans for seedlings and young plants

More sophisticated plantarium

Holes for ventilation (c. 3 cm in diameter)

Special strip lights

Sliding glass panes on either side

Heating by means of special cable

Ventilation

Heating cables at bottom of plantarium

This plantarium is equipped with a thermostat to control air as well as floor temperature, hygrometer, electric atomizer, min-max-thermometer

drop during the night. Even if the temperatures near the window are lower than in the rest of the room it is advisable to house these orchids in another room with an average temperature of about 12 °C (53 °F). In the choice of plants heat is decidedly the limiting factor.

Never expose the plants to draughts for these can be so very damaging, especially when outside temperatures are very low. The presence of curtains can create many problems: although they are a real hindrance to the orchid-grower no self-respecting housewife would be without them. However they do act as a temperature break and may be handy when plants have to be kept cool during their resting period.

The installation of strip lights (fluorescent tubes) can be very beneficial to window sill orchids. Certain species could never even be cultivated without them and the flowering of many others is helped greatly by their presence. A more detailed discussion of strip lighting will be found in the section dealing with plant windows (p. 52).

The indoor greenhouse ('plantarium')

Plants, if they can only be grown indoors, grow much better in confined spaces away from the detrimental micro-climatic variations of

50

the living room. Moreover they are protected from dust and tobacco-smoke. Since the installation of a plant window is not always possible or desirable a glazed container inside the room is worth considering.

It is difficult to find a suitable name for this type of container: the Germans aptly call it a *Pflanzenvitrine*, glazed plant-cabinet: some people call it a tropicarium, but this is rather pretentious and presupposes the presence of other tropical plants in very highly simulated environmental conditions. A proprietary name for such an indoor 'mini'-greenhouse is a plantarium, and this apt term will be used in the rest of this book. There is no limit in size—from very small containers in the one-roomed flat to really large structures suitable for public rooms in a hotel or the banqueting hall of a stately home. They have, however, to be custom built, though there is also plenty of scope here for the home handyman and do-it-yourself enthusiast. Since the plantarium does not receive much daylight a good artificial lighting system is of paramount importance. An efficient air exchange system is also necessary because, although draughts are to be deplored, the effects of damp, stagnant air are probably even more harmful.

A larger plantarium can become the focal point of a room, rivalling a favourite piece of furniture or

51

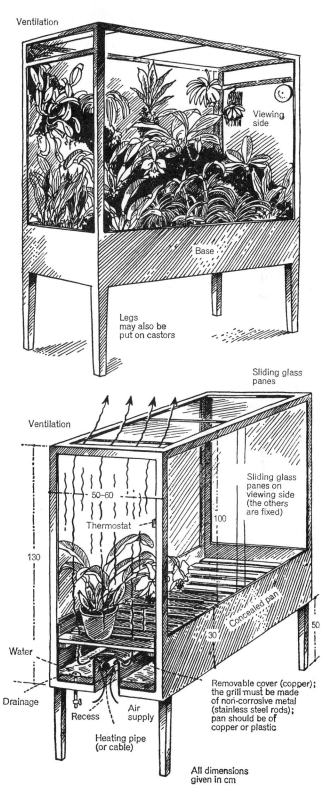

Plantarium specially designed for tropical orchids, allowing for growth (design Ernst Linz)

Ventilation

Viewing side

Base

Legs may also be put on castors

Sliding glass panes

Ventilation

50–60

Thermostat

Sliding glass panes on viewing side (the others are fixed)

130

100

Concealed pan

Water

30

50

Drainage

Recess

Air supply

Heating pipe (or cable)

Removable cover (copper); the grill must be made of non-corrosive metal (stainless steel rods); pan should be of copper or plastic

All dimensions given in cm

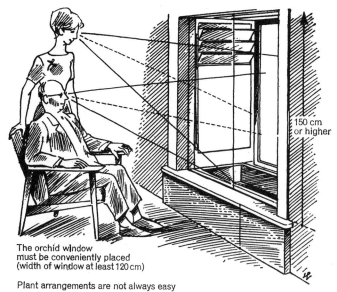

The orchid window
must be conveniently placed
(width of window at least 120 cm)

150 cm
or higher

Plant arrangements are not always easy

Ask the professional for advice

Inside bay

Bay window

Often too warm
and dry

Often too cold
or too hot
in sunny positions

But more recommended than this:

even the television set! It can also be used as a suitable room divider and in this case its aesthetic value is even greater, but as most orchids in the non-flowering state are rather dull and uninteresting it may be worth including a few other plants.

In the ideal plantarium the environmental conditions are automatically controlled: this permits the prolonged absence of the orchid enthusiast, as when he is on holiday, without undue damage to the plants. However, with automatic control, the range of plants suitable for any one set of conditions is limited. There is still no real substitute for individual attention.

Since the plantarium has many problems in common with the plant window the reader is advised to read the following section also.

The plant window

For a plant window to be a real success careful thought must be given to its situation, construction and perhaps above all the choice and arrangement of the plants within it. The technical equipment is also most important.

It is difficult to determine what really constitutes a plant window. In Britain they are still very rare; there are more in America, but they are really a feature of many houses in countries of continental Europe,

52

especially in Germany and Holland. In a new building the architect must be asked to make provision for including such a structure in a suitable place. To build it on to an existing window limits its size and shape and, moreover, planning permission from the local authority is necessary.

The windows vary from being merely a glazed window box to a large glazed section of a room, which may even extend into the ground outside. Although their architectural features are important, they are basically functional structures rather than aesthetic additions.

Plant windows fall into two distinct categories. The simplest form has no glass between it and the room on to which it is built and in in fact is really little more than a specialized version of a window sill. Although this is the most usual form it is not very suitable for orchid culture as the plants are subject to the vagaries of the atmosphere of the room. This handicap is eliminated in the second category where a glass partition divides the window from the actual room. The glass partition is provided either by a hinged or sliding glass, or glazed door. This type of picture window guarantees more or less constant conditions although the partitioning off from the room means that it must have its own heating system. The dimensions are dictated by the house itself

53

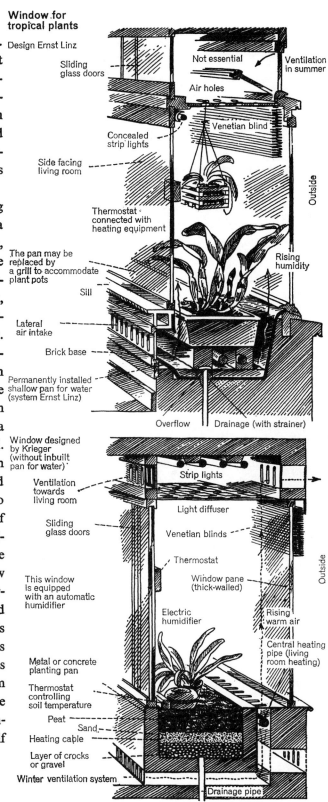

Window for tropical plants

Design Ernst Linz

Sliding glass doors

Not essential

Ventilation in summer

Air holes

Concealed strip lights

Venetian blind

Side facing living room

Thermostat connected with heating equipment

Outside

The pan may be replaced by a grill to accommodate plant pots

Rising humidity

Sill

Lateral air intake

Brick base

Permanently installed shallow pan for water (system Ernst Linz)

Overflow

Drainage (with strainer)

Window designed by Krieger (without inbuilt pan for water)

Strip lights

Ventilation towards living room

Light diffuser

Sliding glass doors

Venetian blinds

Thermostat

This window is equipped with an automatic humidifier

Window pane (thick-walled)

Electric humidifier

Rising warm air

Central heating pipe (living room heating)

Metal or concrete planting pan

Thermostat controlling soil temperature

Peat

Sand

Heating cable

Layer of crocks or gravel

Winter ventilation system

Drainage pipe

Outside

but it should, ideally, be not less than 1 m (3 ft) wide and have a minimum height of 1.2 m (4ft) in order to house the taller orchids. Generally speaking, the larger the window the greater the effect. The lower level is again governed by the structure of the house but with a new house the architect can plan it as you wish, provided local building regulations are not infringed. Most plants should not be above the eye-level of persons seated in the room and this means a lower level of no more than 50–70 cm (20–28 in.) above floor level. To take full advantage of the different light and temperature régimes within a single plant window as well as of the space available, orchid plants can be suspended from the top or sides as well as placed at the bottom of the window. It is not advisable to divide the window horizontally by shelving, even if the shelves are made of glass, because the light absorption by the shelves would make conditions at the lower levels intolerable for most plants. As far as the depth of the picture window is concerned it should be at least 30–40 cm (12–16 in.) but should not exceed 90 cm (36 in.), though in any case this latter size may be structurally impossible.

It may be possible to construct a picture window in a bay window and this has the great advantage of better lighting although there is the considerable disadvantage of a greater heat loss in winter.

A deep tray is very useful at the bottom of the structure not so much for planting in but as a humidity regulation device. This tray should be filled with peat or small gravel or pebbles and should be kept more or less moist. Another method of maintaining humidity is to pave the base of the window with absorbent stones, but if this is done the plant pots should be placed on saucers to prevent excessive water accumulation and stagnation. As with window boxes, humidity may also be maintained by having shallow water-filled trays at the base of the window and placing the pots containing the plants on clay pots inverted in the water. This method, however, is not very acceptable aesthetically.

The actual position of the window should be governed by the same considerations as those which apply when siting window boxes, but as the heating system of the former is less dependent on outside factors, picture windows can also face northwest, north or northeast. This is quite advantageous for certain orchids, such as those from moist mist forests, where the conditions are usually cooler and more constant. Examples include such well known species as *Odontoglossum crispum* and many of the more popular miniatures and botanicals.

There is a danger with picture windows that face the sun: their totally enclosed nature and relatively small air space may lead to overheating and irreparable damage to the occupants. Shading, therefore, is very necessary and should be applied before any overheating starts. Another method of preventing overheating is partial ventilation, the ventilators being situated between the window and the room. Various shading devices have already been mentioned in connection with window box culture but I will again emphasize that such devices are preferable on the outside so that the sun's rays can be 'dispersed' before they enter the picture window. It must also be stressed that as soon as the sun's rays lose their midday intensities the shading should be reduced because a lack of light can do almost as much damage as the overheating caused by too much radiation. Smaller plant windows are especially vulnerable to overheating and excessive humidity, in the same way as plantaria. The correct balance between light and heat requirements can be met by well controlled ventilation. Plants need fresh air just like everybody else!

Ventilation can come either entirely from the inside (from the living room) or from the outside air as well. However the temperature differences between outside air and plant window may be so great that disasters could occur. If outside air is used it should never be allowed to come into direct contact with orchid plants in the window.

In the colder season the window will need additional heating. Ideally this would be supplied by a specially designed radiator, though a pipe from the house central heating system would be sufficient. Again, however, caution must be exercised and the upward current of warmer air from the radiator must not be allowed to damage the plants. Electric cable warming is also very suitable and can easily be installed by the do-it-yourself enthusiast although the completed installation should be checked by the electricity authority. For a smaller plant window the heat produced by an ordinary domestic tungsten light bulb could be sufficient to maintain a moderate temperature. Infra-red lamps are not suitable since they only heat surfaces and not the surrounding air.

Whatever heating is eventually decided upon it can either be controlled manually according to the thermometer or automatically by the installation of a thermostat. When a thermostat is used great care must be taken to keep it in good condition and fully operative and accurate as a malfunctioning one, especially when the owner is absent for a time, can cause disastrous losses. In the high temperatures and humidity of a plant window a thermostat, although perfectly adequate for a living room may corrode rapidly and give false readings: it may need replacing quite frequently.

In larger windows where there is a considerable thermal gradient between the top and bottom, the thermostat, or the thermometer if the temperature is manually controlled, should be situated at the height of the top of the uppermost plants. It is even better to have two thermometers placed at the top and bottom of the window. Once the thermal gradient has been determined the planting of different species can be more accurately carried out.

At least during the darker months of the year an additional source of light is required. Artificial lighting, unobtrusively and tastefully installed, considerably

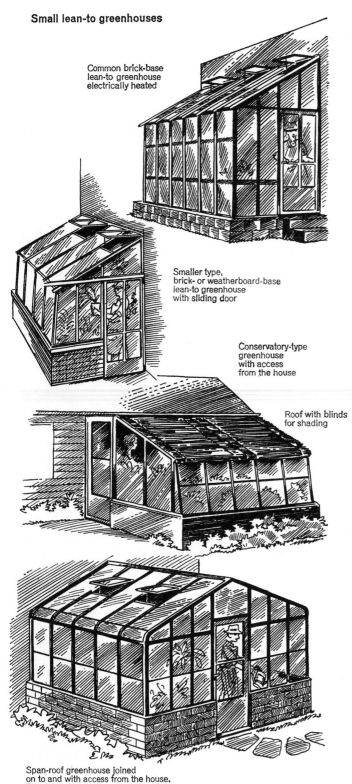

Common brick-base
lean-to greenhouse
electrically heated

Smaller type,
brick- or weatherboard-base
lean-to greenhouse
with sliding door

Conservatory-type
greenhouse
with access
from the house

Roof with blinds
for shading

Span-roof greenhouse joined
on to and with access from the house.
This type of greenhouse is extendible

enhances the aesthetic appeal of the plant window. Fluorescent tube lighting is preferable for the well-being of the plants as the possibility of excessive heating and consequent scorching is reduced but it is not very pleasing artistically, having an excessively functional appearance and a tendency to glare, though the latter can be overcome with light diffusers as illustrated on p. 53.

The duration of the artificial lighting each day should vary with the position of the picture window and with the time of the year. Between 6 and 10 hours of artificial light per day has been shown, by trial and error, to be suitable for most purposes. Much longer periods of artificial lighting are not necessarily damaging provided that a dark spell at night is assured. Ordinary tungsten lighting is cheap to install but does not compare favourably with strip lighting because of the relatively short guaranteed life of the bulbs, about 1000 hours. Strip lights on the other hand usually last for 7500 hours. Recently tungsten bulbs with a longer life have been introduced commercially but their efficacy has not been proved for plant growth and, in any case, they are more expensive to buy and give less light for the amount of electricity consumed. All tungsten bulbs have a much higher electricity consumption rate than fluorescent tubes and they can produce excessive heat.

56

1 Phalaenopsis 'Amphytrion'; 2 Phalaenopsis equestris; 3 Phalaenopsis mannii; 4 Doritaenopsis 'Little Gem'; 5 Doritis pulcherrima var. buyssoniana; 6 Phalaenopsis lueddemanniana var. hieroglyphica

1 Interior of amateur's lean-to greenhouse; **2** Orchids on the balcony during summer; **3** Plant window before planting; **4** Same window with plants in position

The greenhouse

For the cultivation of orchids a greenhouse is the most suitable environment and to possess one should be the ultimate ambition of all those who now grow their plants on window sills or in plantaria and picture windows. The greatest advantage of an outside greenhouse is that light is not only provided laterally but also from above. Also, since greenhouses are larger than the other indoor structures, temperatures and humidity are more accurately controllable and, of course, more plants can be grown! To many orchid enthusiasts a greenhouse has one overwhelming advantage and that is that it is possible to potter about, as well as seriously maintain the plants, without fear of the effects of these operations on the furniture, the floors and the family.

Of course there are also disadvantages in owning a greenhouse and the most serious one is the high cost of installation and maintenance. The time necessary to maintain the greenhouse and its occupants in good condition can also be a disadvantage: a passion for caring for

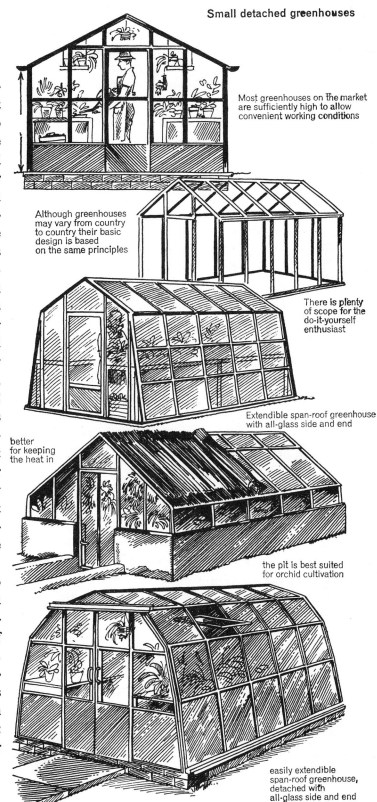

Most greenhouses on the market are sufficiently high to allow convenient working conditions

Although greenhouses may vary from country to country their basic design is based on the same principles

There is plenty of scope for the do-it-yourself enthusiast

Extendible span-roof greenhouse with all-glass side and end

better for keeping the heat in

the pit is best suited for orchid cultivation

easily extendible span-roof greenhouse, detached with all-glass side and end

59

orchids must not become a drudgery. Furthermore, heating a greenhouse adequately in winter can be a great problem. If, for example, it is heated by an extension from the central heating system of the house, the lower temperature supplied at night by most such systems can be dangerous to the greenhouse. It is better to have an independent heating system. An electrical heating system is ideal as it requires little maintenance time and is easily controlled by thermostats but the initial cost and running costs, especially for commercial growers, can be very high indeed.

Some gardeners use their greenhouse, at least as far as orchids are concerned, solely as a 'convalescent home' for those plants normally grown indoors but the great majority use them throughout the year.

Above all a rational and dependable heating system is necessary. There is an optimal size for a greenhouse: the largest ones are too expensive to heat, and a large proportion of the volume they enclose is unoccupied by plants; the smaller ones are more difficult to control as far as heat loss is concerned and can cool down and, incidentally, heat up too rapidly. If a thermostat fails, as it might during a cut in the electricity supply, the smaller houses suffer very considerably and the results of a lifetime's care and devotion may be destroyed overnight. It is desirable to position the greenhouse as close to your house as possible, so that access is not difficult during cold weather (although a 'lean-to' type structure is not entirely satisfactory).

The directional positioning of the greenhouse is subject to the same considerations as those governing the situating of plant windows. Ideally an east-west position is the best and a north-south one is to be avoided if possible. Undue reflected heat and shading from neighbouring buildings and trees should be avoided.

There are numerous firms in Britain and the United States making and supplying greenhouses; nearly all advertise widely either in the national newspapers or gardening magazines. The price range is enormous but, generally, as with so many items, you get what you pay for. Basically the greenhouses offered are of aluminium, galvanized steel, hard wood or cedar wood construction and may or may not be already glazed. In any case the construction of a greenhouse by the rawest amateur, from the semi-prefabricated structures usually available from the majority of firms, is not difficult. The only materials not usually supplied are the bricks for the foundations and low walls. If money is no object it is best to purchase a greenhouse specially designed for orchids and several firms sell these. The much cheaper, more mass-produced structures are, however, perfectly adequate. All are well made and with the minimum of attention can last a lifetime. A very recent development worthy of the attention of orchid growers is the circular greenhouse, which is offered by several firms.

There are two basic types of greenhouse suitable for orchid culture: the sunken house, or 'pit' and the more normal structure.

The pit (see p. 59) usually has low unwindowed walls which bear the roof, the bench surface is at ground level and the central path is sunk into the ground. The heating pipes run parallel with the low walls and the control of temperature and humidity is not difficult. Pits are most suitable for those species which favour a cooler moister atmosphere e.g. Paphiopedilums, Masdevallias, Odontoglossums and Lycastes, but they are also quite adequate for those species demanding much higher temperatures, such as Cattleyas and Vandas. Unfortunately pits are expensive to buy and very expensive to install.

The modern trend is to grow orchids in an ordinary greenhouse with glazed sides, either right down to the ground or on a low brick, asbestos or wooden side wall. The central path is at ground level and the slatted benches are at normal table height. Such a greenhouse is more airy and lighter than a pit but these advantages are somewhat outweighed by the danger of heat loss and the greater difficulty in maintaining adequate humidity. However, with sophisticated heating control systems and manual or automatic 'damping down' these faults can be rectified. A most desirable greenhouse is one that is double glazed and the excessive cost of purchasing one is eventually outweighed by the lower cost of heating.

Intermediate between the greenhouse and the picture window is the glazed verandah or 'conservatory'. Although most orchids can be grown in a conservatory it is best suited for plants requiring cooler conditions or for those in the resting state.

Orchids in the basement

In the tropical regions of the world orchid growing is simplicity itself since there is no need for any special structure in which to house the plants, except possibly a lath house to ward off the sun's rays at the hottest time of the day. In the temperate zone I have shown how orchids can be grown in and around the house but always in a special structure such as a plant window or greenhouse. However there are some parts of the world where orchids can be grown successfully out-of-doors during the summer months but where, because of the low winter temperatures, they have to be taken inside at the onset of autumn when the temperature at night sinks below 10°C (50°F). A suitable place in which to house these orchids during the unfavourable season is in a basement or cellar provided it is well ventilated but not draughty and has some sort of heating.

Ideally the room should be painted white throughout and the benches on which the plants are housed should be about 110 cm (43 in.) above floor level. About 70 cm (28 in.) above bench level fluorescent strip lights should be fixed, with fully functional reflectors if at all possible. The leaves of the average plant will then be about 10 cm (3 in.) away from the light source which should provide about 13 000 to 18 000 lux. Humidity can be obtained from strategically placed gravel-filled pans kept constantly wet. If possible an electric humidifier should be installed as well as a small ventilator to prevent stagnation of the air. If there is a small window or other ventilation device such as a hatch or a door this should be kept fully operational for the admission of fresh air and especially so that the night temperature may drop about 7°C (45 °F), a drop which appears to be necessary for many species growing in these conditions. The plants should usually be sprayed once a day and watered when necessary. The lights, humidifier and electric ventilator should be switched on at about 6 every morning and a time switch is recommended for this. After about fourteen hours, the light should be turned off and outside air admitted if not too cold and not liable to cause a draught. Except for a negligible amount of heat from the fluorescent tubes the only heat will be from the back flow pipes of the central heating system. In December the light must be reduced to 12 hours daily but gradually increased to $13^1/_2$ hours daily until the plants are reintroduced to the garden in mid-May.

It is not possible in most parts of Europe to grow orchids out-of-doors at any time of the year without the protection of a greenhouse. However it may still be worth experimenting if your climate basically resembles that of the warmer parts of the United States, though great care must be exercised at the time of transferring the plants out-of-doors so that the sun does not scorch the leaves or cause premature bud drop.

From reports on this new mode of culture it would appear that the plants maintain excellent health in the basement environment, probably because of the constantly maintained level of light.

CARING FOR ORCHIDS

One of the most important points to ascertain when caring for orchids is whether or not they would be subject to seasonal changes in their native haunts. Some orchids come from the humid tropics where seasonal alterations in light, temperature, rainfall and humidity are very small but many other species are used to considerable seasonal fluctuations. For these latter species, which probably comprise the great majority of cultivated orchids, the growing period usually starts imperceptibly at the end of the year. In the greenhouse, even at the beginning of January under good internal and external conditions, the roots begin to develop and the first sight can be had of new flower buds. As the days lengthen, growth hastens, reaching its climax during the summer months. When autumn approaches the plant matures and ripens its pseudobulbs and then enters the resting phase.

Maximum amounts of light, air and water, both atmospheric humidity and compost dampness, are necessary during the period of maximum growth. Light intensity can be fairly critical for optimal growth and the plants should be placed in position of sun, half-shade and full shade accordingly. Only when grown under ideal conditions will they eventually ripen their bulbs properly and be ready for good growth the following year.

During the resting periods temperatures should be somewhat lower and dampness and humidity reduced. The active processes of life are thereby considerably slowed down but, as in the hibernation of animals, respiration does not completely cease. Light is reduced because of the shorter days but tropical orchids soon adjust themselves to these conditions which do not exist in the tropics. Plants should be prepared for their resting period gradually: this means a gradual reduction of the application of water and a slow lowering of heat. Nevertheless this ripening programme must not be adhered to if flowers are still open or are in the developing stage.

With certain species where new buds and new vegetative growths appear separately at different times of the year another resting phase may be inserted after flowering and before the new growths appear.

There are also a few species which commence their new growth in autumn itself: they should be repotted when the new shoots are about 10 cm (4 in.) long and during the winter they will still need a certain amount of water.

63

Changing conditions over the year

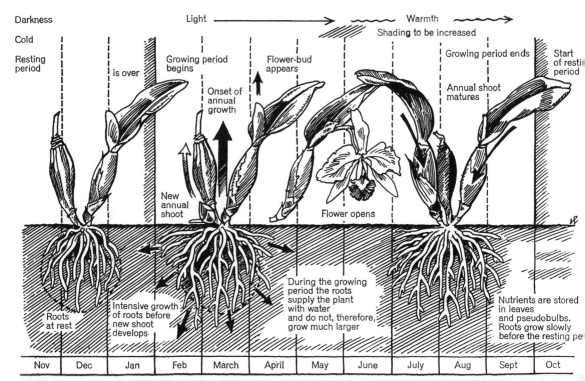

Spring-flowering Cattleyas set flowers on old shoot; those which flower in the autumn or in winter set them on the new annual shoot.

In the case of even more specialized plants like Calanthe and Catasetum which actually drop their leaves at the end of the growing period, a well marked resting period is really essential and with Calanthe it should be noted that this definite resting period should not be started until the flowers have appeared. With Calanthe and Catasetum it is essential that the resting pseudobulbs are kept dry and very light in order to prevent the precocious development of new growths.

If there are no true food and water reserve organs such as pseudobulbs or tubers but the leaves are thick and fleshy enough to maintain the plant during occasional droughts the plants should be kept slightly cooler (10–15°C, 50–59°F) and very little water should be given in the resting period although the compost should never be allowed to dry up completely. In the case of genera such as Vanda and Paphiopedilum where there are no true storage organs of any type whatsoever, the amount of water given and the temperatures should only be marginally reduced during winter.

With Phalaenopsis especially, the leaves must never be allowed to shrivel and die because of a lack of water at the roots.

64

GROWTH FACTORS

As mentioned previously these are basically light, temperature and humidity but now we must also mention mineral requirements. The role of these factors has already been stressed but in the following account they will be dealt with in greater detail and their interdependence emphasized.

Light

Fundamentally, increasing amounts of light lead to increasing growth rates but eventually an optimum light intensity is reached at which growth is at a maximum and higher light intensities will only lead to the eventual damage of the more vulnerable parts of the plant. In natural conditions in the orchid's native haunts, light is accompanied by heat also radiated from the sun. From their precarious perches high at the tops of jungle trees many epiphytic orchids can withstand what would appear to be excessive light intensities and heat radiation because of the ever-flowing currents of cooler, moister air. However in jungle conditions these high light intensities are relatively constant throughout the day and, furthermore, the amounts of light and darkness every twenty-four hours also vary very little throughout the year. These conditions are all quite different from those of temperate regions where even the angle of the sun's rays alters at different seasons.

If orchids were not adaptable plants we should not be able to transfer them to the alien and seemingly inhospitable conditions of the temperate zones and successfully flower them. It must be pointed out nonetheless that because an orchid can withstand certain conditions in the wild it will not necessarily be able to tolerate them in cultivation. For example, the heat produced by high light intensities playing on newly imported orchids through the glass of a greenhouse will tend to scorch or at least severely yellow the leaves. This can be prevented by shading the greenhouse and increasing humidity and ventilation as soon as the plants start to overheat. A rough, but useful, guide is to touch the leaves of an orchid in a greenhouse: if they feel warmer than the surrounding air they could well be in danger and the measures mentioned above should be put into operation.

65

Day-night rhythm in the tropics

day		day		day		day		day		day		day		day		day		day
5.2.		21.2.		5.3.		21.3.		5.4.		21.4.		5.5.		21.5.		5.6.		21.6.	

| Short day | day | | day | | day | | day | | day | | day | | day | | day | | day | Long day |

Day-night rhythm in Central Europe

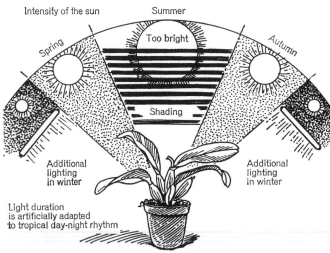

Intensity of the sun — Summer
Spring — Too bright — Autumn
Shading
Additional lighting in winter
Additional lighting in winter
Light duration is artificially adapted to tropical day-night rhythm

The difference of light intensity between winter (too dark) and summer (too bright) can be compensated by artificial lighting or shading

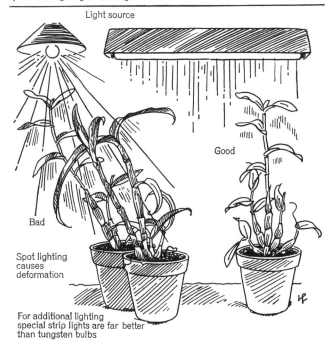

Light source
Good
Bad
Spot lighting causes deformation
For additional lighting special strip lights are far better than tungsten bulbs

At light levels above or below the norm the plant itself will reflect these intensities in various ways. Plants grown in shadier conditions tend to elongate abnormally ('etiolation') whereas under high light intensities growth is often stunted and frequently a red protective coloration develops. The intensity of the greens of an orchid also varies with differing light values.

If there are doubts about the light requirements of any particular orchid it is usually safe to assume that it will grow, and almost certainly thrive, under conditions of semi-shade. Again the sum of one's experience with one's own plants in a particular greenhouse in a particular situation is the best guide.

From the technical literature available it would appear that the most suitable range for orchid growth is 6400 to 3200 lux and this certainly gives a wide margin. Yet not everybody can measure the light intensity in his greenhouse and in fact light readings alone are not always that useful because of the important effects of temperature and humidity, all three factors working very closely in conjunction with each other.

66

The seasons also have to be considered: the sudden increase in strength of the sun's rays as spring comes round can be detrimental to all orchid plants that have spent the winter with very little light. Therefore shading must be provided in the spring and throughout the summer. Neither should it be reduced too much at the end of the summer because even the early autumn sun can damage new buds and shoots. Nearby trees can provide an automatic shading device! When the leaves appear on the trees in spring they offer good shade and when more light is required at the end of the summer they start to shed their leaves.

Stunted growth or even the complete lack of new shoots are sure indications of insufficient light over a long period. Even on normally grown plants the shoots produced during the darker, shorter days are smaller and more stunted than those produced in summer, and this again is a direct result of the quantity, and probably quality, of light. This lack of light in winter can be compensated for by artificial lighting which, as mentioned earlier, enables many species to be grown indoors that could not otherwise be considered. It is always tempting to experiment with the growing of supposedly difficult species by altering the light régime, but orchids are usually too costly to

67

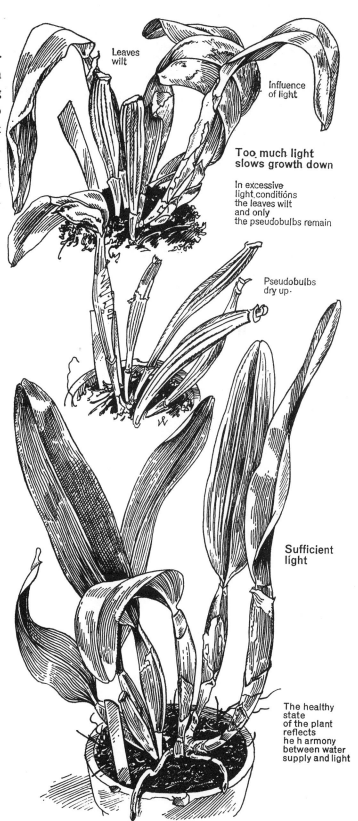

Leaves wilt

Influence of light

Too much light slows growth down

In excessive light conditions the leaves wilt and only the pseudobulbs remain

Pseudobulbs dry up.

Sufficient light

The healthy state of the plant reflects he h armony between water supply and light

risk failures! Probably because of this we still know very little about the light requirements of many of our cultivated orchids.

According to Dr Gustav Schoser, the Director of the Palmengarten at Frankfurt, (German Federal Republic), the following light requirements have proved successful:

Cattleya and relatives

after germination	2 000 lux 16 hrs/day
after pricking out	4 000 lux 16 hrs/day
4 cm (2 in.) pot	6–15 000 lux 16 hrs/day
8 cm (4 in.) pot	up to 25 000 lux 16 hrs/day

If the light is increased to 45 000 lux the first flowering of many species can be brought forward very considerably.

Cymbidium, Odontoglossum and hybrids

seedlings, all stages	8 000 lux 16 hrs/day
older plants	15 000 lux 16 hrs/day

Paphiopedilum

seedlings	2 500 lux 16 hrs/day
older plants	7 500 lux 16 hrs/day

Phalaenopsis

seedlings	1 000 lux 12 hrs/day
older plants	7 500 lux 9 hrs/day

To provide these light conditions about 40 watts of tungsten light per square metre are required for the lowest values; 400 watts per square metre for 10 000 lux and proportionally more for the higher values.

Outside the darker period of the year lights are only required for the seedling stages.

As it would be difficult and costly for the average amateur to provide the above mentioned ranges of lights a compromise is obviously necessary. In average greenhouse conditions about 100 watts of tungsten lights per square metre will suffice whereas in the less favourable environment of an indoor greenhouse perhaps 200 watts per square metre for sixteen hours per day would be ideal.

Only strip lighting should really be considered and the advantages and reasons have already been stressed on p. 50.

The quality of the light is also most important and by quality we mean the relative amounts of the different colours in the spectrum. Specially colour-balanced fluorescent tubes are available and these provide the correct colours for optimum chlorophyll development and photosynthesis. Unfortunately these lights are not very pleasing aesthetically and again a compromise with more normal lighting is suggested for indoor cultivation.

Temperature

By the hereditary impress of generations every plant is adapted to a certain range of temperatures. This really means that it will only perform the functions of its life cycle optimally within a relatively narrow tolerance. If plants are grown outside these limits poor growth or even death will result. Again it must be stressed that temperature, light and humidity work very much in conjunction with one another and unless a harmonious relationship is achieved optimum growth is not possible in any case. With low humidity high temperatures can be dangerous with too much atmospheric moisture the effects of low temperatures can be emphasized. A widely held misconception is that all tropical orchids need really high temperatures: this is not altogether true and to subject them to such treatment can be disastrous. In the very early days of orchid cultivation the many failures were due entirely to trying to grow orchids in the excessive temperatures of the 'stove' house.

Three basic temperature régimes enable the enthusiast to grow nearly all cultivatable orchids. They are the cold or cool, the intermediate, sometimes called temperate, and the warm, or hot.

Cool

summer

| day | 16–21 °C | (61–70°F) |
| night | c. 13 °C | (c. 55°F) |

winter

| day | 13–16°C | (55–61 °F) |
| night | c. 10°C | (c. 50°F) |

In these conditions many Cymbidiums, Odontoglossums, Paphiopedilums and Zygopetalums will thrive.

Intermediate

summer

| day | 18–24°C | (64–75°F) |
| night | 16–18°C | (61–65°F) |

69

winter

| day | 16–21 °C | (61–70 °F) |
| night | 13–16 °C | (55–61 °F) |

Cattleyas, Laelias, Oncidiums, Stanhopeas and Dendrobiums, especially those of the latter genus from the Himalayan region, are suitable for the intermediate house.

Warm

summer

| day | 21–29 °C | (70–84° F) |
| night | 18–21 °C | (65–70 °F) |

winter

| day | 21–29 °C | (70–84 °F) |
| night | 18–21 °C | (65–70 °F) |

Here winter and summer temperatures should be kept fairly similar. Under thess conditions Phalaenopsis, some Paphiopedilums and the evergreen Dendrobiume will thrive.

For further information on the temperature requirements of individual species see pp. 152–181.

Although these temperatures should be adhered to as far as possible it is almost impossible for the amateur to avoid higher temperatures at midday in mid-summer and lower temperatures during winter nights, but if these extremes exist only for a relatively short period well grown plants will not suffer. For example, warm house orchids can quite safely be lowered to 12 °C (53 °F) without harm, provided there is not too much humidity. However, in all cases temperature changes must not be too sudden and must not occur too often.

As with light, young plants require rather more heat but not too much!

For heating apparatus reference should be made to earlier sections especially pp. 55 and 60.

Humidity and moisture

We must distinguish between the humidity of the atmosphere and the moisture content of the potting medium whether it is soil, a compost of osmunda or other natural fibre, or even of inert plastic material.

Humidity, which is very important for the good growth of all plants especially tropical ones and particularly epiphytes, is much more difficult to control than either heat or light. It has been proved that about 50 per cent humidity is suitable for most orchids.

When orchids are grown on window sills or in the open plant window they are largely at the mercy of the humidity of the general atmosphere. This varies very greatly from area to area and from country to country and it would be unwise to generalize. However local meteorological records and newspaper weather reports can always be consulted and if the general humidity is low steps can be taken to remedy it, as mentioned on p. 44.

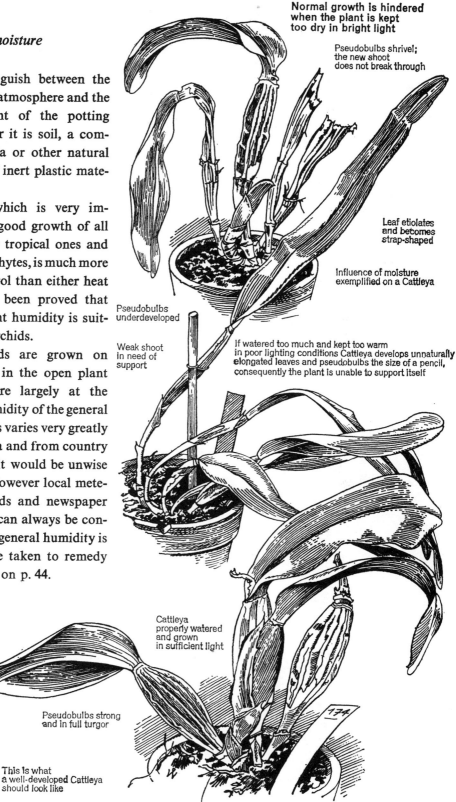

Normal growth is hindered when the plant is kept too dry in bright light

Pseudobulbs shrivel; the new shoot does not break through

Leaf etiolates and becomes strap-shaped

Influence of moisture exemplified on a Cattleya

Pseudobulbs underdeveloped

Weak shoot in need of support

If watered too much and kept too warm in poor lighting conditions Cattleya develops unnaturally elongated leaves and pseudobulbs the size of a pencil, consequently the plant is unable to support itself

Cattleya properly watered and grown in sufficient light

Leaves well-shaped, tough and deep green

Pseudobulbs strong and in full turgor

This is what a well-developed Cattleya should look like

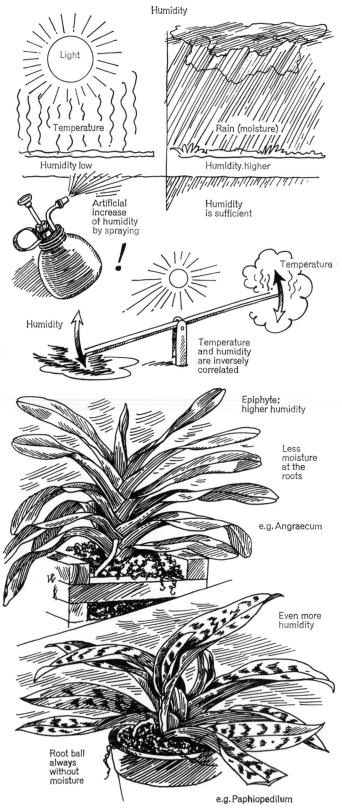

Light

Humidity

Temperature

Rain (moisture)

Humidity low

Humidity.higher

Artificial increase of humidity by spraying

Humidity is sufficient

!

Temperature

Humidity

Temperature and humidity are inversely correlated

Epiphyte: higher humidity

Less moisture at the roots

e.g. Angraecum

Even more humidity

Root ball always without moisture

e.g. Paphiopedilum

It must be stressed again that temperature and light should also be taken into consideration when deciding to increase local humidity.

In the greenhouse or plant window humidity can be increased most effectively by an atomizer, but spraying the surfaces can be almost as effective.

In the stagnant air of a greenhouse it is wise to reduce humidity at night—this is in complete contrast to natural conditions where the moisture content of the air is usually much greater during darkness but where it is counteracted by air movements which are absent from the greenhouse.

As a general rule, any form of watering, damping down, or spraying should not be performed in the late afternoon or evening (although it must be recognized that several growers obtain excellent results by doing just this! If there is high humidity in the greenhouse towards the end of the day the falling temperatures at this time cause condensation and plants will become covered with a film of water droplets which can be quite damaging.

Correct watering is one of the greatest problems of orchid cultivation. There is a direct relationship between atmospheric humidity and compost moisture. Fundamentally the lower the atmospheric humidity the damper should be the compost, and the higher the humi-

72

dity the lower the moisture content of the potting medium. It is better both from the plant's viewpoint and from the general maintenance of the greenhouse to aim at higher humidities, by spraying and damping down, and less watering of pots.

In any case excessive moisture at the roots can be very damaging and low air moisture content can cause irreparable damage to young leaves and flower buds. A potting medium should never be wet but just evenly moist. Occasionally short term drying-out is beneficial as this closely imitates natural conditions whereby epiphytes are subject to very dry spells. Although it is not advisible to water pots daily they should all be examined frequently and if too dry well watered or even submerged by total dipping. Terrestrial orchids require more water than epiphytes and only in the case of species with a very well marked resting period should the soil be allowed to dry out completely.

For the special requirements of certain plants such as species of Paphiopedilum see pp. 142–151, 176 to 177. To judge correctly when a plant needs watering experience is the only guide. Although the surface of the compost may be perfectly dry the lower levels may still be rather wet. Beginners tend to overwater their plants and as a general rule too much moisture is far more damaging than too little.

73

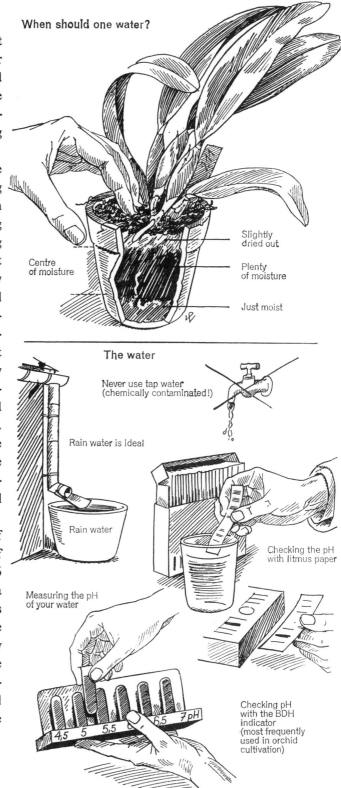

When should one water?

Slightly dried out

Centre of moisture

Plenty of moisture

Just moist

The water

Never use tap water (chemically contaminated!)

Rain water is ideal

Rain water

Checking the pH with litmus paper

Measuring the pH of your water

Checking pH with the BDH indicator (most frequently used in orchid cultivation)

4,5   5   5,5   6   6,5   7 pH

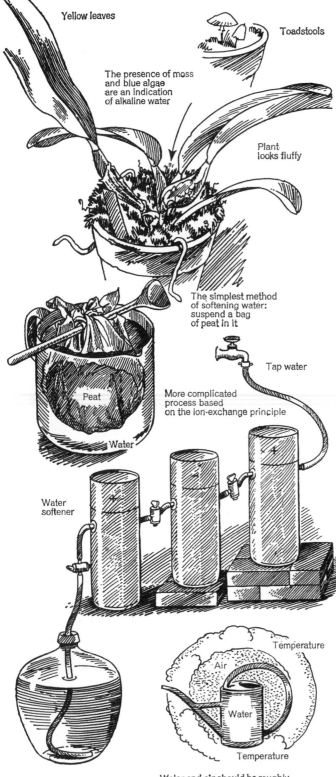

Yellow leaves

Toadstools

The presence of moss and blue algae are an indication of alkaline water

Plant looks fluffy

The simplest method of softening water: suspend a bag of peat in it

Tap water

More complicated process based on the ion-exchange principle

Peat

Water

Water softener

Temperature

Air

Water

Temperature

Water and air should be roughly the same temperature

The quality of water used, whether it is for spraying, damping down or watering direct, is of great importance. Since tap water has usually been chemically treated, generally with elemental chlorine, it should be used with caution. Especially important is the degree of acidity or alkalinity of the water. This is expressed as the pH ('potential Hydrogen'), a pH reading of 7 being neutral, above 7 is alkaline and below is acid. For best results orchids need a slightly acid water of about pH 5.

The degree of hardness of the water has also to be taken into consideration. This depends on the type of soil and rock through which the water has percolated after it has fallen as rain. For orchid cultivation no more than 4° hardness should be tolerated. Since it is very difficult for the amateur to ascertain the amount of hardness in the local water supply it is advisable to obtain information from the Local Authority or Water Board.

The best water is undoubtedly rainwater except in areas with a high degree of atmospheric pollution, which is common in industrial areas and in older style high density housing. Rainwater, as it passes through the air, absorbs and dissolves many substances such as dust, pollen and other organic matter. It is this enriched rainwater that contributes towards the nutri-

74

1 Interior of orchid 'pit'; 2 Detached greenhouse

1 Odontoglossum 'Royal Sovereign'; 2 Cattleya labiata

ment of plants. These solutes also affect the pH of the water and this must be measured frequently. The simplest way of doing this is with litmus paper. As far as the well-being of plants is concerned small changes of pH are not very damaging, many orchids are still quite happy up to pH 7. Rainwater also contains a certain amount of dissolved air and especially important for plants are carbon dioxide and ammonia. To maintain a well-balanced flora and fauna of micro-organisms the rainwater should also contain a good proportion of oxygen. Stagnant water is poor in this element and should be avoided if at all possible. An abnormal population of soil micro-organisms, such as is caused by too little oxygen in the soil water, can cause the wrong type of decay of waste organic matter and this can lead to the destruction of the compost and of the orchid plant itself.

As it is not possible to store a sufficiently large quantity of freshly aerated rain water, it can be revitalized by pumping air into it with an aquarium aerator.

If, by misadventure, too alkaline water is applied (and this can easily be recognized by the presence of blue-green algae on the surface of the compost), the effects may be minimized by adding a phosphate (1 : 1000) solution. If there is an excessive growth of algae it is better to wash the compost thoroughly or even to discard it completely and repot the plant.

Where only very hard water is available it must be softened by a chemical water softener. Although chemical water softeners have been in domestic use for many years great improvements have recently been made in the field of ion-exchange chemistry. Modern water softeners require very little maintenance and labour but can be rather expensive to install. However, as this softened water contains little or no nutritious mineral matter it is not advisable to use it exclusively for watering. On the other hand it does enable one to control most accurately the feeding of one's plants.

Finally the temperature of the water is important. If the water temperature and surrounding air temperature are equal no harm will result and slight differences either way can be tolerated by healthy plants. Fatal, or long term damage not easily discernible at first, can result from watering with too cold water.

Feeding

Whether or not to feed orchid plants has long been a controversial question. Until quite recently the general consensus of opinion was that it was not necessary and could in fact be dangerous. The advent of new, inert, plastic potting materials may, however, necessitate the feeding of plants. If in doubt the beginner should not feed but rely on rainwater to supply his plants' needs.

Three basic principles apply to orchid feeding: only well rooted plants should be fed; the feed is preferable in small but frequent doses; and it should only be applied during the period of maximum active growth. The actual feed can be organic or inorganic.

Organic Feeding

The use of organic fertilizers seems obvious since they are the natural food of orchids. Unfortunately, however, the precise chemical formulae of organic feeds are not usually known and it is therefore impossible to control accurately a plant's intake.

The best mixture is prepared by steeping any or all of the following: cow- or pigeon-dung, dried blood, hoof and horn, in water. (Exact quantities cannot be stipulated—personal experience is the only guide!) When fermentation has finished the liquid should be strained and diluted to the colour of pale tea. If pigeon-dung is used more or less exclusively, since it is very rich in nitrogen, phosphate and potash at a concentration of about 1 : 1000 should be added to it. Nevertheless, as natural as it is, the application of organic feeds has a great disadvantage in that it decomposes the potting compost very quickly.

There are several commercial organic feeds on the market and many of these are good for orchids, especially those prepared from fish or seaweed bases.

Inorganic Feeding

With inorganic feeding the exact proportions of the different chemicals can be accurately ascertained and the plants fed according to their requirements. The essential elements are nitrogen (N), phosphorus (P), and potassium (K). K is mainly responsible for the control of flower- and fruit-development, P for flower production and N for healthy vegetative growth. The amount of feeding depends on the plant concerned, the time of year and general health of the plant. Investigations have shown that feeding should begin with more N just when the new shoots are showing, more P and K being necessary towards the end of the season.

The following scheme has been suggested:

Mature plants

Season	Dosage	N P K
March–May	0.05% every 3–4 weeks	2 : 1 : 1
June–August	0.1% every 2 weeks	2 : 1 : 1
September–October	0.1% every 2 weeks	1 : 1 : 1

Young plants

All seasons   0.05% at regular
                     intervals   3 : 1 : 1

Requirements for inorganic feeding and the tolerance against excessive amounts are correlated but much feeding is done by trial and error. The order from highest to lowest in terms of requirements for the commoner genera is Cymbidium, Phalaenopsis, Dendrobium and Cattleya. Intolerant of inorganic feeding are Paphiopedilums and even organic feeds are best avoided with plants of this genus. Although inorganic feeds are usually given in liquid form it is possible to dry-feed and the addition of dried blood and bonemeal is often practised especially when dealing with Cymbidium, Coelogyne, Lycaste, etc.

Cattleya (for example)
is repotted every second year

The decisive factor
is the state
of the plant

Around
the middle
of March

New shoot   New roots

This plant should be repotted

Repotting

Without compelling reasons orchids should not be repotted! If,
however, aeration of the potting
material is poor because of decomposition it must be replaced. If in
doubt, put it off for another year!
Basically care must be taken that
new growths and shoots are not
overlapping the rim of the pot, for
large neglected plants which have
been potted for a long time are no-
toriously difficult to handle and it
is very easy to break off new shoots
and roots. As to the frequency and
time of repotting there are certain
rules.

Annual Repotting: Calanthe,
Dendrobium phalaenopsis and its
hybrids, Paphiopedilum and Phalaenopsis.

Method

Take plant carefully out of its pot;
don't injure the roots

Carefully remove crocks
from the root ball

Do not re-use
old crocks!

Pot has
become
too small

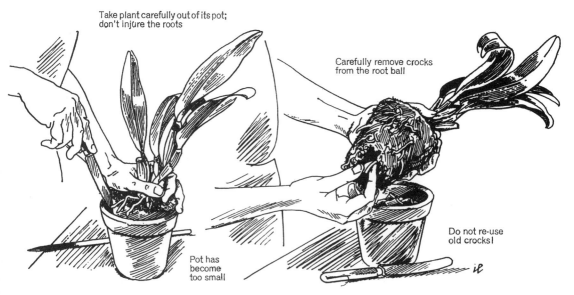

Every other year: Cattleya, Dendrobium, Oncidium and Odontoglossum.

Every third year: Vanda and its allies, Cymbidium.

Less frequently: all 'tussock' orchids.

It must be stressed again that repotting can seriously disturb a plant and therefore should not be undertaken more than necessary.

Repotting times do not vary very much but should usually be at the beginning of the active growing season or at least when the new roots appear, i.e. mid-January to May. For Phalaenopsis this was traditionally done in August but it has since been shown not to be necessary. *Odontoglossum crispum* and its relatives and its hybrids should be repotted in November. Cattleya and its relatives should be repotted when the new shoots are about 5 cm (2 in.) long.

The techniques of repotting can be difficult both for amateurs and professionals and certain rules must be learned, especially regarding the treatment of the roots.

To remove the root-ball from the pot it is advisable to use a knife. All old potting material, dead roots and shrivelled pseudobulbs have to be removed. With sympodial orchids such as Cattleya, Dendro-

81

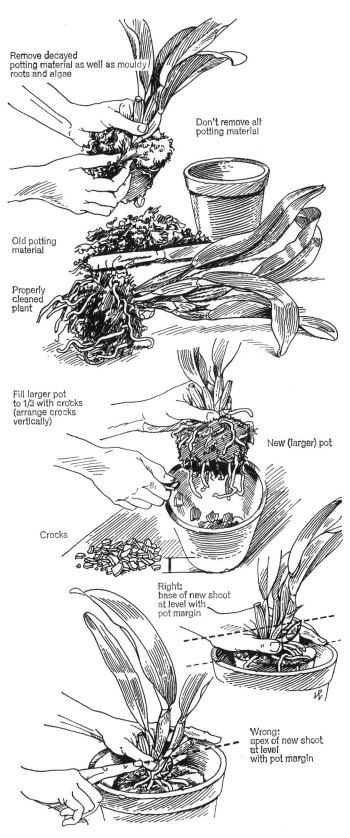

Remove decayed potting material as well as mouldy roots and algae

Don't remove all potting material

Old potting material

Properly cleaned plant

Fill larger pot to 1/3 with crocks (arrange crocks vertically)

New (larger) pot

Crocks

Right: base of new shoot at level with pot margin

Wrong: apex of new shoot at level with pot margin

Repotting

(continued)

Press down potting material by hand

Fresh potting medium

Potting stick

Start pressing down around the edges

Control pressing with left thumb

Test density of potting mixture with both thumbs

bium, Odontoglossum, etc., not more than 5 or less than 3 pseudo-bulbs should remain.

When the older pseudobulbs, the backbulbs, are removed from many orchids it will be noted that they often have 'eyes'. These back-bulbs can be planted in small pots and within 2–3 years will be like or-dinary plants. The containers, pots, pans, baskets or rafts, should be large enough to carry two shoots or developing growths. Too large pots are to be avoided because they can actually retard growth and inhibit flowering.

The pots should be filled to about $\frac{1}{3}$ of their height with broken crocks (in the vertical position) over which a few pieces of charcoal should be sprinkled. The bottoms of baskets should be covered with large flat crocks. The bases, gener-ally the roots of the plants, are then covered with the potting compost and placed in the prepared pots. The oldest pseudobulb should be against the edge of the pot and the youngest ones towards the centre so that there will be ample space for new shoots and pseudobulbs to grow. More potting material is gradually added, being tamped down firmly with a potting-stick working from the outside towards the centre. With a coarse potting medium the top level should be 1–2 cm below pot level. Although the beginner may feel that the repotted plant is

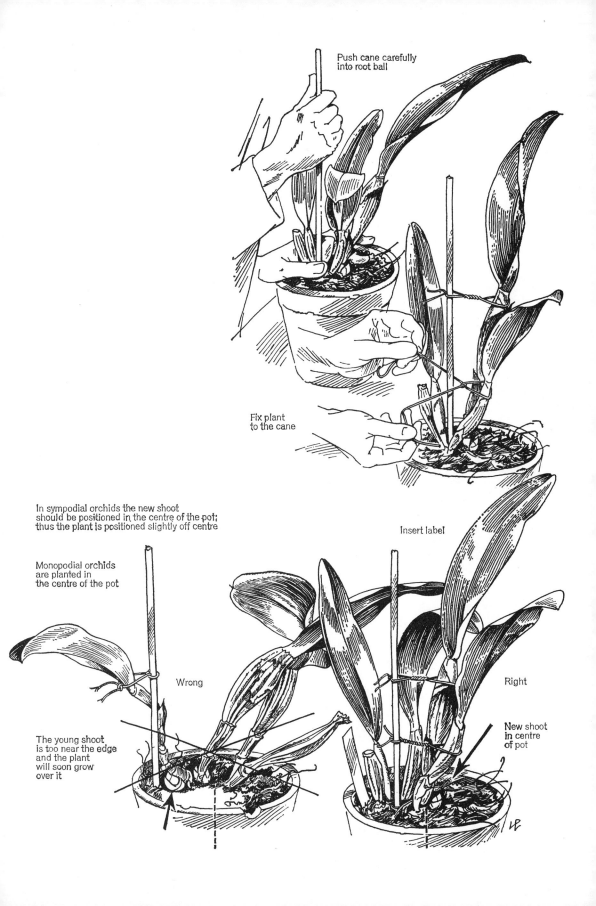

Push cane carefully
into root ball

Fix plant
to the cane

In sympodial orchids the new shoot
should be positioned in the centre of the pot;
thus the plant is positioned slightly off centre

Insert label

Monopodial orchids
are planted in
the centre of the pot

Wrong

Right

The young shoot
is too near the edge
and the plant
will soon grow
over it

New shoot
in centre
of pot

Repotting a plant suffering from a root disease

Plant looks weak and does not grow well

Leaves somewhat wilted; pseudobulbs thin

Remove fungus-infected potting material entirely and cut out damaged roots

Dip roots in solution of disinfectant

Solution of disinfectant

Insert roots carefully into new pot, then press down new potting mixture

²/₃ of the new pot filled with fresh crocks

too 'firmed-down', this is necessary because natural decomposition will eventually loosen it.

Monopodial orchids, such as Vanda, Renanthera and Phalaenopsis, should be potted similarly but, since they do not have pseudobulbs, they should all be planted in the centre of the pots. In Paphiopedilum the potting material is topped up with sphagnum, which, with correct watering, will continue to grow and be beneficial to the plants as well as act as an indicator of the condition of the compost. Extra attention must be paid to recently repotted plants. Damaged roots do not absorb moisture and therefore for the first few weeks after repotting the plants should be sprayed and not watered. Paphiopedilums, however, need watering just after repotting.

As far as raft or block culture is concerned only the mounting has to be explained. The right size of block must first of all be decided upon. If the plant is too large the raft dries out too quickly: on the other hand, a small plant on a very large raft is not aesthetically pleasing. Another factor to consider is the ultimate size of the plant. For the actual planting the roots and perhaps part of the stem should be wrapped in potting material and placed on the raft; then more potting material should be placed on top and the plant firmly fixed to the

84

1 Dendrobium sophronites; 2 Oncidium marshallianum; 3 Cirrhopetalum mastersianum;
4 Epidendrum radicans; 5 Cochlioda noezliana; 6 Habenaria rhodocheila

1 Cymbidium lowianum; **2** Cymbidium Babylon ′Castle Hill′ × C. Alexandri ′Westonbirt′; **3** Renanthera Brookie Chandler; **4** Aërides odorata

1 Gongora galeata; **2** Dendrobium devonianum; **3** Odontoglossum rossii; **4** Oncidium concolor

1 Laelia pumila var. praestans; 2 Dendrobium devonianum; 3 Cattleya citrina; 4 C. bowringiana

raft with plastic covered wire. Plastic string can also be used for fixing but is not desirable. In the course of time the roots will grow and fix themselves firmly to the raft. The further treatment of raft-grown plants is really not different from those grown in the more traditional flower pots. However, since they are more exposed to the air, they tend to dry out more rapidly and need more frequent spraying, watering or even dipping. Besides this, raft plants tend to require more feeding: but this should not be overdone, especially with botanicals and miniatures which are very self sufficient provided they are adequately watered.

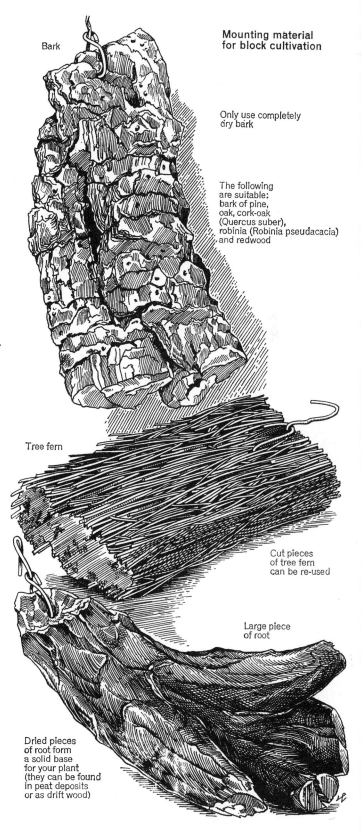

Bark

Mounting material
for block cultivation

Only use completely
dry bark

The following
are suitable:
bark of pine,
oak, cork-oak
(Quercus suber),
robinia (Robinia pseudacacia)
and redwood

Tree fern

Cut pieces
of tree fern
can be re-used

Large piece
of root

Dried pieces
of root form
a solid base
for your plant
(they can be found
in peat deposits
or as drift wood)

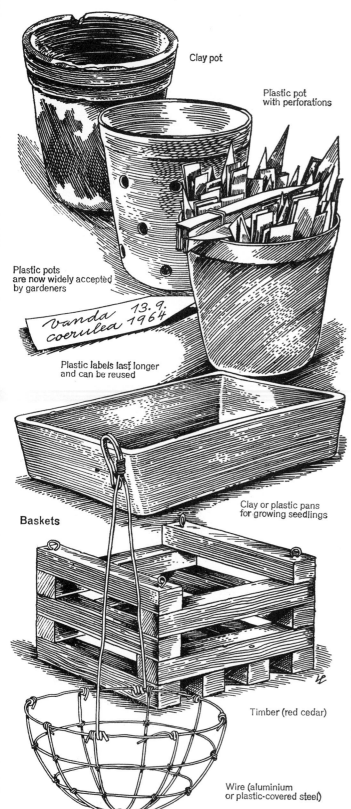

Clay pot

Plastic pot
with perforations

Plastic pots
are now widely accepted
by gardeners

*Vanda 13.9.
coerulea 1964*

Plastic labels last longer
and can be reused

Baskets

Clay or plastic pans
for growing seedlings

Timber (red cedar)

Wire (aluminium
or plastic-covered steel)

Plant Containers

In choosing a suitable type of container, be it pot (of clay or plastic), basket or raft the needs of the plant must be considered along with one's own preferences. Terrestrials present no problems, being grown exclusively in clay or plastic pots or pans (although a modern trend is to experiment with growing them in open beds in the larger greenhouse in a manner similar to that for commercial Cymbidium culture). There is a wider choice of container for epiphytes but basically they can be grown in either pots or baskets, i.e. with their roots covered, or on pieces (rafts) of bark or blocks of osmunda. Raft and block culture is by far the best way for the smaller and more difficult botanicals especially as this method avoids frequent repotting. The bark of the cork oak *(Quercus suber)* is extremely amenable to plant growth as well as being very durable. Ordinary oak or pine bark is not so durable but even so will last for several years. Because of their porosity and durability the stems of tree ferns are also extremely good. Gnarled trunks and branches of vines are often used on the continent of Europe because of their easy availability but especially because of their bizarre shapes. 'Bog oak', i.e. preserved trunks and roots of trees, usually pines, that were overcome

90

Put plant
on growing medium

Surround roots
with growing medium

Block of tree fern

**How to mount orchids
on the block**

Position
plant correctly;
water runs down
from the centre

Wrong:
water collects
in the centre

Fix plant
with wire

Ready:
plant and
growing medium
are properly
in position

91 Imported plant
(Dr Gut Prag, Ghana 64)

by bog growth several thousand years ago but remained in a pickled state almost unaltered structurally until revealed by recently eroding peat bogs, are also very good but there may well be a greater demand for this type of material from the flower-arrangers in the family! If the salt is washed out thoroughly, drift wood, that other great feature of floral artists, is also good for orchid growing. Many other trees yield branches that are suitable provided the bark is left on and particularly good is that from oaks and the false acacia *(Robinia pseudacacia)*.

As far as the mounting of specimens is concerned see p. 91.

In larger collections the traditional clay pots are still used, mainly because of their cheapness. They are also useful for the beginner as indiscretions of over-watering are offset by the porous nature of the pot which, incidentally, also helps to maintain atmospheric humidity. Nevertheless, care must be exercised with clay pots because their porosity leads not only to evaporation but to the under-cooling that accompanies it. There are clay pots made especially for orchid growing and these have additional holes or slits in the sides as well as in the base.

Although plastic pots were at first vehemently rejected by orchid growers, as indeed they were by most horticulturalists, they are now becoming more acceptable particularly since they considerably reduce the task of watering, and, again, special types with additional side and base holes are manufactured for orchid growers.

Expanded polystyrene is very good, especially since its fantastic insulating properties protect the roots and favour their growth but its one great disadvantage is that it is so light that plants are likely to be knocked over more readily. It can fracture and crumble easily, and its aesthetic appeal is also debatable.

The advantage of baskets is that air can enter from all directions, but this can lead to a more rapid drying out of the compost, especially in hot summer spells, and therefore watering is more of a chore with them. Although care must be taken that the innermost layers of compost do not become waterlogged and rotten, the best way of watering baskets is by dipping. The choice of timber for baskets is not very important but to prevent excessive repotting a resistant hardwood is marginally preferable although it may well be more expensive. Oak is suitable but can give off almost lethal amounts of tannic acid. Red cedar is now being tried and appears to be as successful for orchid baskets as it is for greenhouses. Wire baskets, either of galvanized iron or aluminium or plastic-covered copper-wire, can be used and shaped to fashion.

Composts

The great adaptability and vitality of orchids is evident in their ability to show excellent growth when grown in any number of different composts!

The necessary characteristics of the more commonly used composts for epiphytes are discussed below, but one factor stands out as common to all and that is their loose nature, which is essential for the adequate aeration of orchid roots. The material must also be durable and capable of holding and providing the relatively low mineral requirements of orchids. Its pH value must be constant and an innate 'buffering' ability must be present to maintain this value. Finally it must be resilient yet springy enough to support the plant adequately without undue ramming and tamping down when potting. No single medium has all these properties and therefore the most successful ones should be a mixture. The ratio of different materials used is a point hotly debated by all orchid growers.

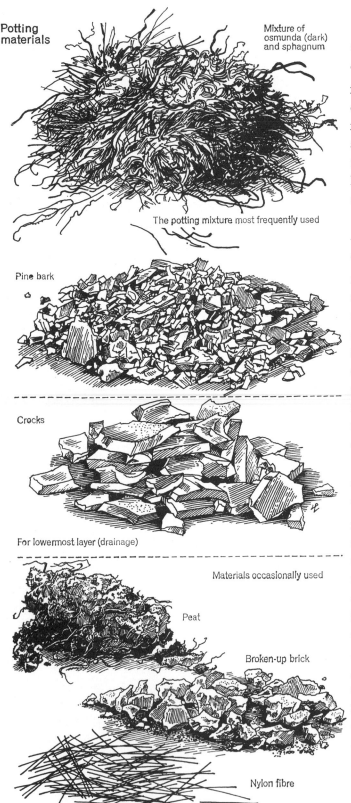

Potting materials

Mixture of osmunda (dark) and sphagnum

The potting mixture most frequently used

Pine bark

Crocks

For lowermost layer (drainage)

Materials occasionally used

Peat

Broken-up brick

Nylon fibre

Osmunda

This is the root fibres of the Royal fern, *Osmunda regalis*. It is hard, durable, sufficiently springy but rigid enough for good anchorage and contains very little mineral matter. Its great disadvantage is its high price and today good quality osmunda is almost unobtainable.

Polypodium fibre

This is the root fibres of the common Polypody fern, *Polypodium vulgare*. It is softer and finer than Osmunda fibre and neither so durable nor as good for anchorage and aeration. A little soil should be added to it and this obviously also increases its mineral content. It is difficult to obtain commercially and tends to be used only for the more delicate miniatures.

Sphagnum

This is the generic name for the bog mosses of which there are many species found all over the world although only at higher elevations in the tropics. All can be used for orchid growing and most can be found in considerable quantities. However the less acid species such as *S. squarrosum* and *S. palustre* are generally considered to be the most suitable. Although it rots rather readily and, when collected wild may contain contaminants such as slugs and snails, it has the advantages

94

of being cheap, of having excellent water retention properties and being quite inert chemically. It is usually used mixed with some other media but can be used by itself for the establishing of seedlings and newly imported plants that need special attention.

Beech leaves
If kept dry after collection, that is, not used in the form of leaf-mould, about 20 per cent added to epiphytic and terrestrial mixtures is very beneficial.

The above mentioned media are the traditional potting composts but difficulties in the supply and cost of some of them has made it necessary to experiment with and evaluate the properties of newer materials.

Tree fern
This is usually obtainable as the ground-down trunks of tree ferns. It is hard, fairly durable, without mineral content and not very expensive but the fibres are not always long and springy enough to provide good anchorage.

Fir bark
The bark of many conifers can be used if cut up and variously shredded into suitable sizes. It is relatively cheap, has good water-retention properties but does not last as long as some of the other materials. However it can be used for rapidly growing species which would tend to outgrow their pots before the fir-bark rots down and becomes sour.

Peat
Coarse fibrous peat, often commercially sold as 'orchid peat' is very good and has the advantage of being readily obtainable and quite cheap.

Synthetic materials
Many plastic materials are now being used. Some, such as those in granular form, are especially manufactured for orchid growing but the more usual fibrous and shredded flake types are the waste ends and off-cuts from various plastic manufacturing processes. The fibrous forms are especially good and may be odd lengths of nylon monofilaments (fishing line) or of a raffia-like appearance, being manufactured basically as a string or baler twine substitute. All these synthetic materials are very durable, being chemically inert and mineral free, are very cheap to buy and sufficiently springy to give good anchorage. However they are best used in conjunction with natural materials so that at least a little mineral matter will be available and some water retained in the compost.

Other materials
Broken brick, pumice granules, gravel and broken coke can either be used by themselves in a form of hydroponic orchid culture or mixed with sphagnum.

95

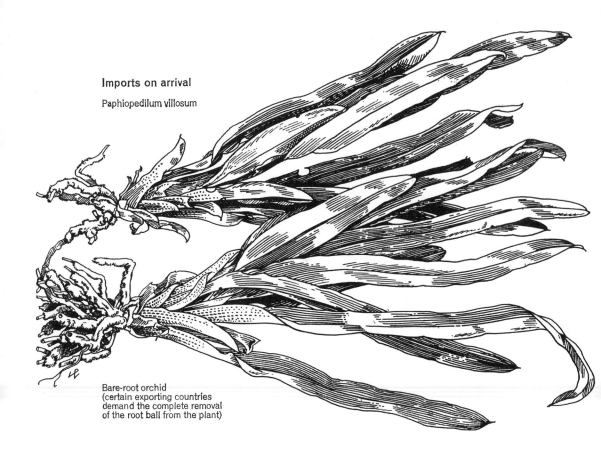

Imports on arrival

Paphiopedilum villosum

Bare-root orchid
(certain exporting countries
demand the complete removal
of the root ball from the plant)

Treatment of newly imported plants

In the early days of orchid growing in Europe and north America the only source
of plants was from those collected in the wild and then imported. Few survived but
those that did formed the basis of the commercial orchid growing industry. Tales
of hundreds of thousands of mature plants of a single species being imported in one
consignment are commonplace and so too is the fact that more than once all were
found to be dead on arrival. This veritable rape of the jungles continues today and
is helped considerably by the great improvements in air transport. Many species are
nearly extinct and it is hoped that in the near future international agreements will
be signed, completely prohibiting the export, import and transit of wild collected
orchid plants except by certain selected licence holders, such as nurserymen requiring new 'blood' for hybridization programmes and artificial propagation and
botanical expeditions completing floral surveys of unknown areas.

96

1 Cattleya aclandiae; 2 Lealia anceps; 3 Cattleya forbesii; 4 C. violacea;
5 C. warscewiczii 'van Houtte' × C. warneri 'Ardenholms'; 6 Laeliocattleya 'Odessa'

Imported orchids for cultivation; **1** Cattleyas on arrival; **2** Specimen of *Cattleya skinneri*; **3** Oncidium *phymatochilum*; **4** *Oncidium leucochilum* already established; **5** Paphiopedilum *callosum* on arrival; **6** same already established; **7** Specimen of *Nageliella* on arrival; **8** Block culture of botanicals

Nevertheless at the moment such wild collected plants can still be purchased and plants are also readily obtainable from nurseries in the tropics where they are grown in semi-wild conditions.

When you receive such plants the first thing to do is to cut off all damaged parts and check for any pest-infested or diseased parts that have escaped inspection at the port of entry. Large tussocks are best divided but not into too small portions without main shoots. They should either be potted up into small pots in a 1 : 1, osmunda : sphagnum, mixture, or laid in boxes and covered with sphagnum. At first they should only be lightly sprayed, never watered or dipped, and should be given plenty of air and shade. Soon they will start to adapt themselves to the surrounding conditions and the roots will begin to grow again. Very often flowering will soon occur and in any case they will usually bloom in less than a year from importation. But the first consideration should be to build-up the plants and, although it may be excessively painful (to the grower not the plant!), the flower-buds should be removed for the first season.

Because of the possibility of frost damage in transit it is advisable not to purchase any orchids from the tropical regions during winter months.

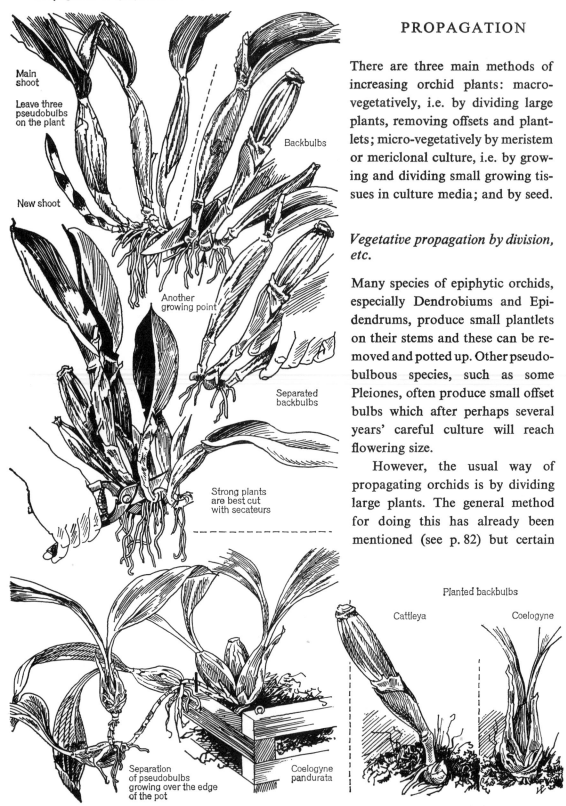

Main shoot

Leave three pseudobulbs on the plant

New shoot

Backbulbs

Another growing point

Separated backbulbs

Strong plants are best cut with secateurs

Separation of pseudobulbs growing over the edge of the pot

Coelogyne pandurata

Planted backbulbs

Cattleya

Coelogyne

PROPAGATION

There are three main methods of increasing orchid plants: macro-vegetatively, i.e. by dividing large plants, removing offsets and plantlets; micro-vegetatively by meristem or mericlonal culture, i.e. by growing and dividing small growing tissues in culture media; and by seed.

Vegetative propagation by division, etc.

Many species of epiphytic orchids, especially Dendrobiums and Epidendrums, produce small plantlets on their stems and these can be removed and potted up. Other pseudobulbous species, such as some Pleiones, often produce small offset bulbs which after perhaps several years' careful culture will reach flowering size.

However, the usual way of propagating orchids is by dividing large plants. The general method for doing this has already been mentioned (see p. 82) but certain

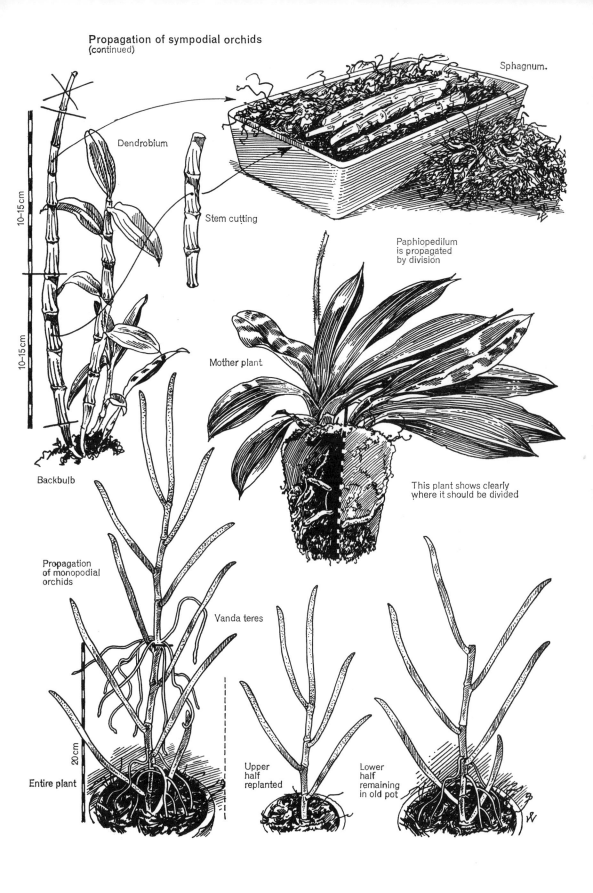

Propagation of sympodial orchids
(continued)

Sphagnum.

Dendrobium

10-15 cm

10-15 cm

Stem cutting

Backbulb

Paphiopedilum
is propagated
by division

Mother plant

This plant shows clearly
where it should be divided

Propagation
of monopodial
orchids

Vanda teres

20 cm

Entire plant

Upper
half
replanted

Lower
half
remaining
in old pot

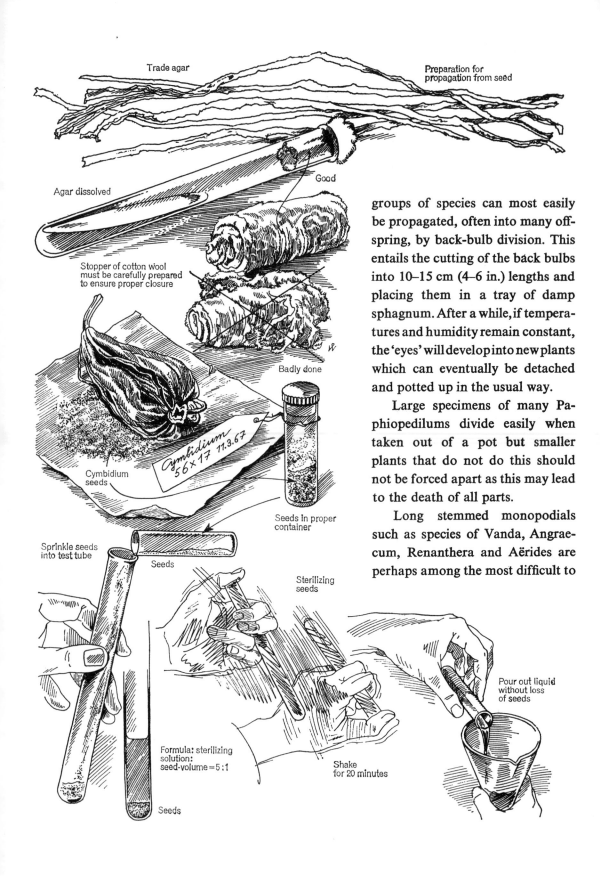

Trade agar

Preparation for propagation from seed

Good

Agar dissolved

Stopper of cotton wool must be carefully prepared to ensure proper closure

Badly done

Cymbidium 56 × 17 11.3.67

Cymbidium seeds

Seeds in proper container

Sprinkle seeds into test tube

Seeds

Sterilizing seeds

Formula: sterilizing solution: seed-volume = 5 : 1

Shake for 20 minutes

Pour out liquid without loss of seeds

Seeds

groups of species can most easily be propagated, often into many offspring, by back-bulb division. This entails the cutting of the back bulbs into 10–15 cm (4–6 in.) lengths and placing them in a tray of damp sphagnum. After a while, if temperatures and humidity remain constant, the 'eyes' will develop into new plants which can eventually be detached and potted up in the usual way.

Large specimens of many Paphiopedilums divide easily when taken out of a pot but smaller plants that do not do this should not be forced apart as this may lead to the death of all parts.

Long stemmed monopodials such as species of Vanda, Angraecum, Renanthera and Aërides are perhaps among the most difficult to

Sowing
with special equipment

Holder

Seeds

Spirit burner

Conical flask containing growing medium

Sowing
with simple equipment

(most frequently done in this fashion)

Spatula

To observe sterile conditions for the sowing process one needs more than average skill and a good deal of patience; cleanliness is of paramount importance

Seed container

The mouth of both glasses must be held over steam

Test tube with growing medium

Sterile method of sowing

Right!

Hot plate

Wrong!

Mouth of glass not over steam!

Wrong!

If test tube is in upright position with its mouth not over steam bacteria will easily get into it

Transfer seeds into test tube

This operation takes place over steam

With spatula take seeds out of container and sprinkle on to the growing medium

Seeds in container

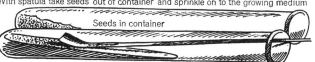

Distribute seeds evenly on surface of growing medium

divide. Only older healthy plants that have developed aerial roots 20 cm (8 in.) or more from their bases should be dealt with by cutting them into pieces below each root. The severed piece, along with its roots, forms a new plant and the original plant, rid of most of its aerial roots, soon develops more roots and will flower probably within three years.

Propagation by seed

Although growing orchids from seed is a delicate and complex operation which most amateurs are advised to shun, leaving it to the professionals, it is perhaps one of the most compelling aspects of orchid culture. In other plant families the sense of personal involvement with germination is negligible because it all takes place in the dark confines of the

103

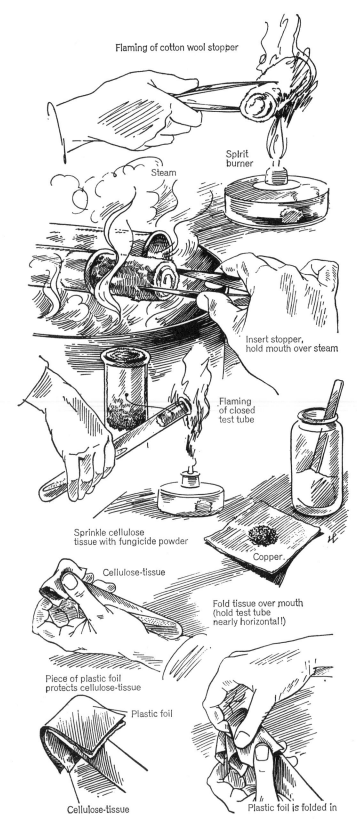

Flaming of cotton wool stopper

Spirit burner

Steam

Insert stopper, hold mouth over steam

Flaming of closed test tube

Sprinkle cellulose tissue with fungicide powder

Copper.

Cellulose-tissue

Fold tissue over mouth (hold test tube nearly horizontal!)

Piece of plastic foil protects cellulose-tissue

Plastic foil

Cellulose-tissue

Plastic foil is folded in

soil but with orchids the seeds germinate in full view of the grower and a feeling of personal responsibility is inevitable. The ultimate ambition in orchid growing is to raise flowering plants from seed but success is not easy. Patience, persistence, very 'green fingers', and an unflappable approach to failure, are always necessary.

There is a peculiar interdependency between orchids and fungi as has been pointed out on p. 6. A brief knowledge of this 'mycorrhizal relationship' is very necessary to understand the procedures of orchid seed germination. There have been developed two distinct and basic methods of germination based on this knowledge. In the first it is assumed that the presence of the fungus is necessary for successful germination. The fungus is isolated, grown in sterile cultures and then, when fully developed in the medium, orchids are sown. This is a time-consuming method which is hardly ever used today. Generally the second, the asymbiotic method, is applied. Here the growing medium is enriched by mineral nutrients which provide the plant with basically the same substances as the fungus. A high degree of sterility, both of the sowing media and the seed is necessary There are many new recipes for suitable germinating media but basically the two original formulae of Burgeff and Knudson are used.

104

ORIGINAL EG-I SOLUTION (Burgeff)

A Calcium nitrate   1.00 g

   Ammonium sulphate   0.25 g

   Magnesium sulphate   0.25 g

   Ferrous sulphate   0.02 g

   Distilled water   500 ml

B Monopotassium acid
    phosphate   0.25 g

   Dipotassium acid
    phosphate   0.25 g

   Distilled water   500 ml

Solutions A and B, after being prepared separately, are mixed and to the mixture is added:

   Sugar   20.00 g

   Agar   15.00 g

pH C. 5.

ORIGINAL SOLUTION (Knudson)

Monopotassium acid
    phosphate   0.25 g

Calcium nitrate   1.00 g

Ammonium sulphate   0.50 g

Magnesium sulphate   0.25 g

Ferric phosphate   0.05 g

Sucrose   20.00 g

Agar   17.50 g

Distilled water   1000 ml

pH adjusted to 5 with hydrochloric acid.

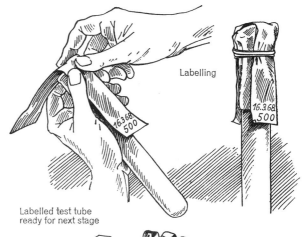

Labelling

Labelled test tube ready for next stage

16.3.68
500

Aquarium used as incubator

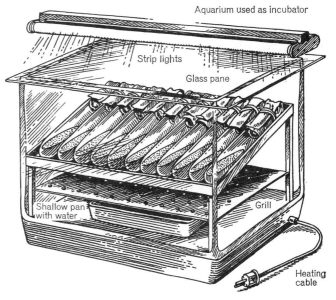

Strip lights

Glass pane

Shallow pan with water

Grill

Heating cable

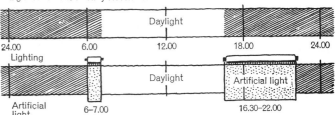

Light conditions in early November

Daylight

24.00   6.00   12.00   18.00   24.00

Lighting

Artificial light   6–7.00   Daylight   Artificial light   16.30–22.00

Further development

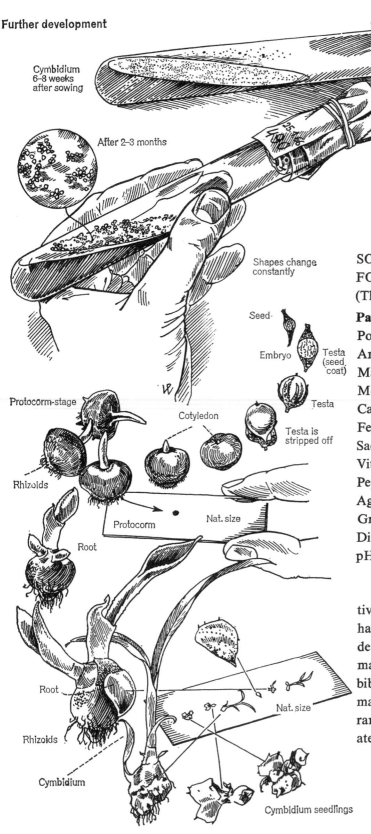

Cymbidium
6–8 weeks
after sowing

After 2–3 months

The time taken from seed
to flower-bearing plant
varies greatly in orchids;
it takes several years
in any event

Shapes change
constantly

Seed

Embryo

Testa
(seed
coat)

Testa

Testa is
stripped off

Cotyledon

Protocorm-stage

Rhizoids

Protocorm

Nat. size

Root

Root

Rhizoids

Nat. size

Cymbidium

Cymbidium seedlings

SOLUTION
FOR PAPHIOPEDILUM
(Thomale-Detert)

Paphiopedilum recipe (Thomale)

Potassium nitrate	0.250 g
Ammonium sulphate	0.050 g
Magnesium sulphate	0.200 g
Mono-calcium phosphate	0.180 g
Calcium sulphate	0.080 g
Ferrous sulphate	0.005 g
Saccharose	20.000 g
Vitamin concentrate	1.000 g
Peptone	3.000 g
Agar	15.000 g
Growth substance '66f'	0.100 g
Distilled water	1000.000 g
pH 5–5.2	

There are many inessential additives which do very little except perhaps enhance the growth of the oldest seedlings Reference should be
made to the latest periodicals (see
bibliography) for up-to-date information on these additives which
range from fish emulsion to macer-
ated bananas.

106

Method

Irrespective of which formula is used the basic ingredients, including the water, should all be heated for a short period in order to dissolve the agar. If the heating is carried out too long too much water will be lost and the formulation will therefore no longer be correct. The pH (acidity value) is then checked with litmus or other indicator to make sure it is as near neutral (pH 7) as possible. If it is too acid, add a few drops of very weak sodium hydroxide (caustic soda) or if too alkaline, either some weak nitric or weak sulphuric acid should be added, and the medium tested again. The melted medium is then poured, while still hot, into either large test tubes or conical flasks of up to 500 cc capacity. These are then plugged with cotton-wool which should be cut in such way that although bacteria are excluded gaseous exchange is still possible. Cellulose can be used instead of cotton wool and so too can natural-rubber bungs fitted with either a water trap or cotton wool soaked in picrid acid, as a filter. The vessels should then be sterilized in an autoclave or domestic pressure cooker but great care must be taken to ensure that temperatures do not rise too high otherwise the sugar may break down into caramel which is useless for orchid nutrition. The vessels are then inclined in an oblique position so that the culture medium presents the largest possible surface. When cooled the medium should be of an even consistency, almost like a stiff dessert jelly, and in any case must not be too leathery.

Orchid seeds could be collected in a more or less sterile condition from the unopened capsule and sown immediately but the risk of contamination is great and this method should be avoided. It is far safer to collect seed from an opened capsule and then sterilize it.

There are several ways of sterilizing orchid seeds, the simplest one being as follows. 10 grams of fresh sodium hypochlorite is dissolved in 140 cc of water and then filtered. The seeds are placed in a test tube, a few drops of the sterilizing liquid added, and the whole lot shaken for 10–20 minutes. Then a shallow saucepan, half-filled with water and gently boiling on a stove, is required over which to carry out the actual sowing. Care must be taken that the air above the boiling surface is not subject to fluctuating currents. The test tube of medium and the test tube containing the sterilized seeds should be held in the left hand over this saucepan. By means of a sterile spatula a small quantity of seed is transferred to the medium and the cotton-wool plug replaced immediately. To enhance the sterility the cotton-wool should be briefly 'flamed' before re-insertion. Over this plug a layer of cellulose wadding is added and dusted with a fungicidal powder. The top of the container should then be finally sealed with a piece of plastic or metal foil.

The receptacles should next be stored in suitable containers at about

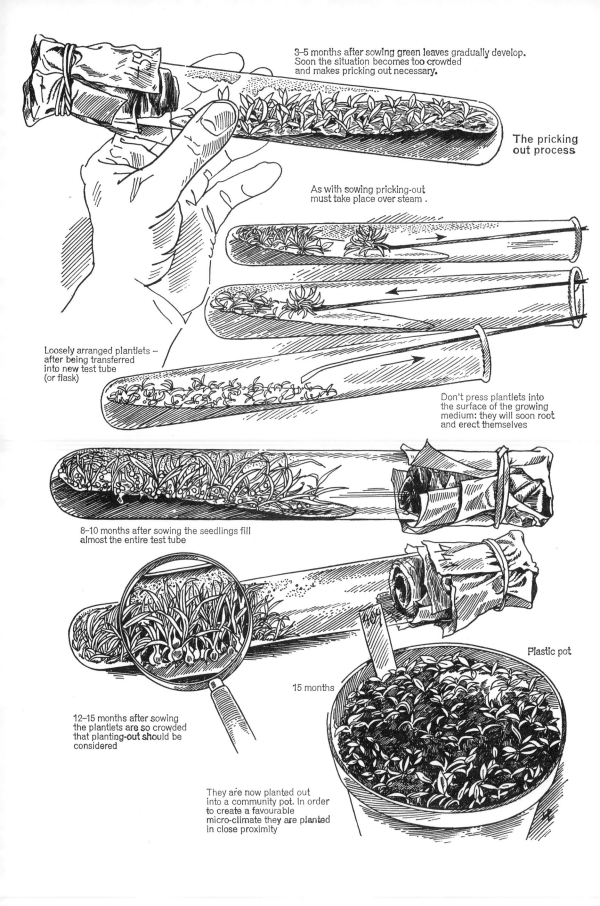

3–5 months after sowing green leaves gradually develop.
Soon the situation becomes too crowded
and makes pricking out necessary.

The pricking out process

As with sowing pricking-out
must take place over steam.

Loosely arranged plantlets –
after being transferred
into new test tube
(or flask)

Don't press plantlets into
the surface of the growing
medium: they will soon root
and erect themselves

8–10 months after sowing the seedlings fill
almost the entire test tube

Plastic pot

15 months

12–15 months after sowing
the plantlets are so crowded
that planting-out should be
considered

They are now planted out
into a community pot. In order
to create a favourable
micro-climate they are planted
in close proximity

Cattleya
19 months old

Pricking-out operation

Lift out seedling

Free roots of
old potting mixture

Arrange seedlings
according to size

Glass
dibber

Use dibber
for making hole

Shape roots to fit easily
into planting hole

Pricking-out
into larger community pot

Result:
Cattleya 24 months old

Insert seedling in planting hole (holding it between thumb and index finger)

Exert slight pressure around seedling

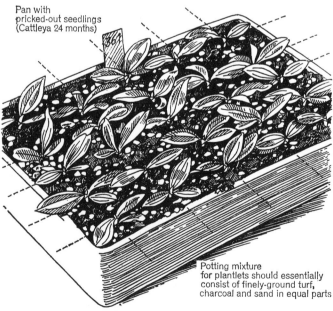

Pan with pricked-out seedlings (Cattleya 24 months)

Potting mixture for plantlets should essentially consist of finely-ground turf, charcoal and sand in equal parts

Although the plantlets stand fairly dense they should be arranged in a certain order to give them an equal chance for development

22°C (71°F) in 60–80 per cent diffused light. To aid germination, especially if a large number of containers are sown at the same time, they should be placed in a glass case with temperature and humidity maintained at an even level. (A pan of water at the base is added to maintain the humidity.) The containers should, however, be kept dry on the outside to minimize the risk of certain bacterial infections. For the same reason they should not be handled unnecessarily.

Germination times vary according to the species concerned. Phalaenopsis and certain Dendrobiums such as *D. phalaenopsis* and *D. bigibbum* take about 10 days; Cattleyas, up to 20 days, and Cymbidiums and Paphiopedilums, as long as 8 weeks.

Further development is much slower and can only be assisted by optimal growing conditions such as are provided by extra light; from dusk to 22.00 hours in the winter and from 6.00 until it is really light in the summer.

The seedlings are called protocorms: they are roundish or 'top'-shaped, and develop fairly fine roots, called rhizoids. After this protocorm stage the single cotyledon and the first proper roots appear. If the seeds were sown too thickly some should be transferred at this stage. If carefully carried out transference should not harm the seedlings.

Transference and pricking out

Usually the seedlings are transferred when they are considerably older and in too close juxtaposition for continued good growth. They are transferred to the same growing medium as originally used and here again sterility must be observed by transferring in a steamy atmosphere. A long spatula would be useful, although care must be taken not to let the plants touch the glass. Often, the denser they are the better they grow and, if possible, they should then stay in this container until ready for planting-out. The correct size and condition of seedlings for planting out depends almost entirely on judgement. Precise dates and sizes cannot be given as so many factors, heat, light, season, etc., can all influence the seedlings' rate of growth. Usually after just less than a year they are all ready for transferring to the open greenhouse.

The substrate into which the plantlets should now be transferred is not just the ordinary potting compost but is specially prepared. It should consist of finely ground turf, charcoal and sand in equal parts and should be kept moderately moist. The 'sweepings' from the potting bench, especially if osmunda has been used, are useful as are also ground-up leaves and fine sphagnum peat. This 'pricking-out' compost should be in shallow

111

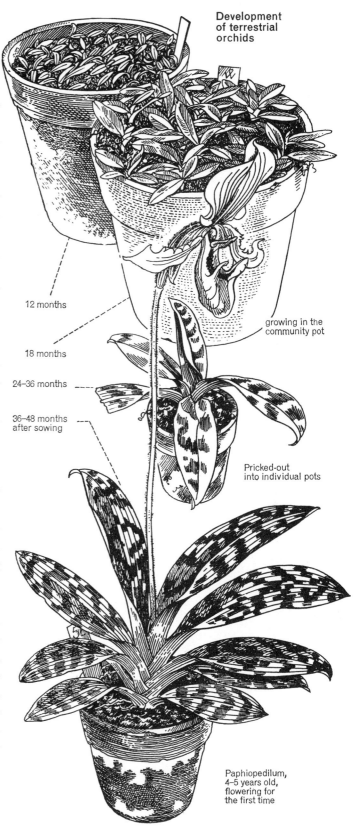

Development
of terrestrial
orchids

12 months

18 months

24–36 months

36–48 months
after sowing

growing in the
community pot

Pricked-out
into individual pots

Paphiopedilum,
4–5 years old,
flowering for
the first time

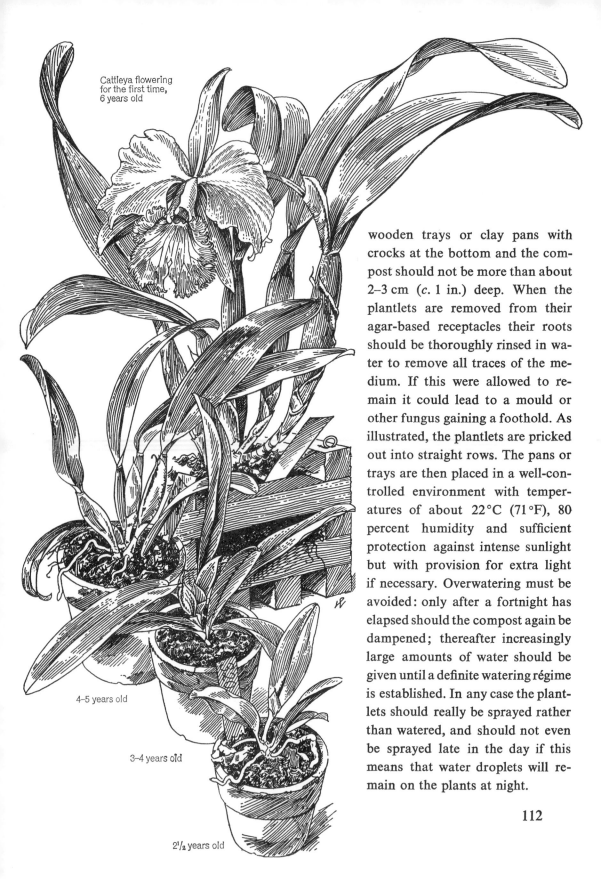

Cattleya flowering
for the first time,
6 years old

4–5 years old

3–4 years old

2½ years old

wooden trays or clay pans with crocks at the bottom and the compost should not be more than about 2–3 cm (*c.* 1 in.) deep. When the plantlets are removed from their agar-based receptacles their roots should be thoroughly rinsed in water to remove all traces of the medium. If this were allowed to remain it could lead to a mould or other fungus gaining a foothold. As illustrated, the plantlets are pricked out into straight rows. The pans or trays are then placed in a well-controlled environment with temperatures of about 22°C (71°F), 80 percent humidity and sufficient protection against intense sunlight but with provision for extra light if necessary. Overwatering must be avoided: only after a fortnight has elapsed should the compost again be dampened; thereafter increasingly large amounts of water should be given until a definite watering régime is established. In any case the plantlets should really be sprayed rather than watered, and should not even be sprayed late in the day if this means that water droplets will remain on the plants at night.

112

The next stage is the planting out into community pots of about 4–5 plants. If they are planted out individually too early they develop much slower. The substrate and care of plants in community pots are the same as for the initial pricking out.

When the plantlets have grown sufficiently large they should be transferred to 5 cm (2 in.) diameter pots. Smaller pots are not recommended but it is in order to plant a few plants in a large community pot. The potting medium at this stage can be the same, basically, as the final one but should be ground up a little finer. Two parts osmunda, one sphagnum and one pine-bark is ideal but even better results are often obtained from a 2 : 1 : 1 : 1 mixture of turf, coke, pine-bark and sphagnum. At this penultimate stage the pot should again be lightly crocked. Do not start watering until it can be seen that root growth is active and in any case do not water for at least a fortnight after repotting. The same general conditions also apply to the yearly repotting. As the plant grows it will need an increasingly larger pot and a coarser potting medium, but never put it into too large a pot. It is always better to under-pot than over-pot. If the grown plant has a well defined resting season this should not be inflicted for a couple of seasons or so.

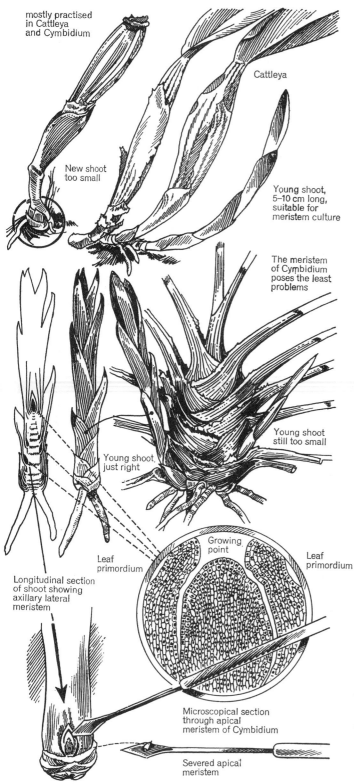

mostly practised
in Cattleya
and Cymbidium

Cattleya

New shoot
too small

Young shoot,
5–10 cm long,
suitable for
meristem culture

The meristem
of Cymbidium
poses the least
problems

Young shoot
still too small

Young shoot,
just right

Leaf
primordium

Growing
point

Leaf
primordium

Longitudinal section
of shoot showing
axillary lateral
meristem

Microscopical section
through apical
meristem of Cymbidium

Severed apical
meristem

Axillary meristem is carefully freed
of its enveloping leaves

Meristem culture

Recently another vegetative repro-
duction method, meristem culture,
has gained importance. The process
is technically very complicated and
demanding and since it also really
requires a laboratory to be carried
out successfully it should not be attempted by any but the keenest,
most patient, and wealthiest, amateurs. However, as it is a method of
great and growing importance, it is
outlined here.

As yet meristem propagation
has only been achieved, to a commercially acceptable standard, in
Cattleya, Cymbidium, Calanthe,
Dendrobium, Miltonia, Odontoglossum, Oncidium, Zygopetalum
and hybrid genera involving these.
Success has not yet been encountered with Paphiopedilum and it
was for a long time thought that
all of the monopodial orchids were
impossible to meristem. However,
Phalaenopsis has recently been me-
ristemmed successfully, and it must
now be simply a matter of time before it is possible to propagate all
orchids in this way, though whether
to a commercial extent or not is
uncertain. Plants produced by this
method are known, when oung,
as mericlones.

The cultivation of living tissues,
plant or animal, outside the parent
organism has been practised for
several decades. In orchids it has

114

1 Paphiopedilum hybrid; **2** Cattleya trianaei 'The Premier';**3** Cattleya warszewiczii 'Frau Melanie Beyrodt'; **4** Cattleya dowiana aurea

1 Paphiopedilum insigne; 2 P. Leyburnense

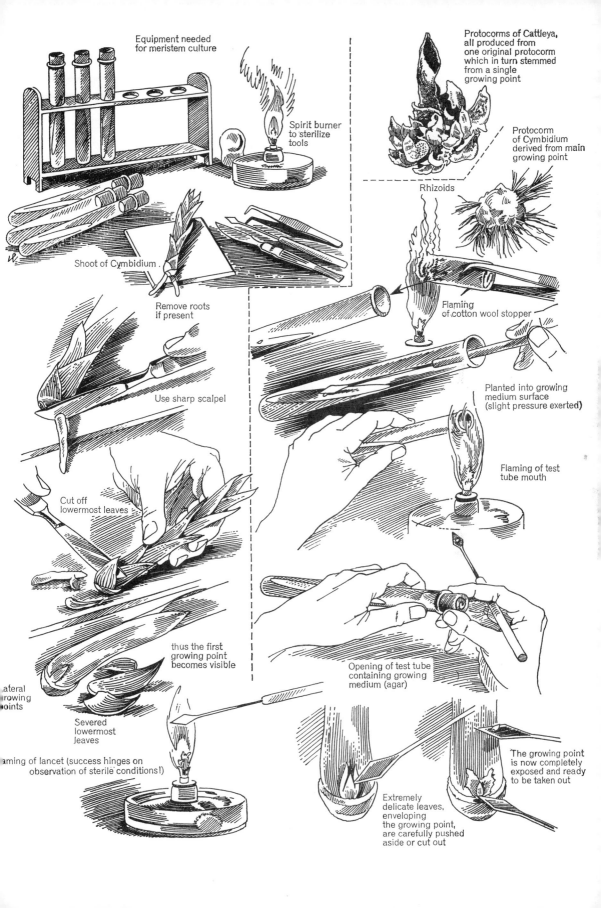

Equipment needed for meristem culture

Spirit burner to sterilize tools

Shoot of Cymbidium.

Protocorms of Cattleya, all produced from one original protocorm which in turn stemmed from a single growing point

Protocorm of Cymbidium derived from main growing point

Rhizoids

Remove roots if present

Use sharp scalpel

Cut off lowermost leaves

thus the first growing point becomes visible

Lateral growing points

Severed lowermost leaves

Flaming of lancet (success hinges on observation of sterile conditions!)

Flaming of cotton wool stopper

Planted into growing medium surface (slight pressure exerted)

Flaming of test tube mouth

Opening of test tube containing growing medium (agar)

Extremely delicate leaves, enveloping the growing point, are carefully pushed aside or cut out

The growing point is now completely exposed and ready to be taken out

been achieved relatively recently. In 1960 the French scientist, Dr Georges Morel, of Versailles, reported successful experiments on the mericlonal propagation of Cymbidium, Phaius, Miltonia and Cattleya. Since then professional scientists and commercial orchid growers have improved their techniques and today it is a great commercial tool. Many hundreds of thousands of identical plants can be produced in a relatively short period from the excised growing point of a single growth. Basically all such propagules from a single meristem should be genetically and morphologically identical but with the increasing numbers produced there are many rumours that 'sports' or mutations have arisen, and this is to be expected. Unfortunately for the nomenclaturalists great problems will arise with these 'sports'.

In all plants there are particular types of cell in which exist the potentialities of the plant. The tissue in which these cells are found is called a meristem and it is found at the extremities of the roots and shoots. In pseudobulbous species the meristem growing period comes to an end at a certain time. The lateral meristems develop at the base of the pseudobulb after a more or less pronounced resting period and from them the meristem shoots again, thus ensuring the survival of the species. The apical meristem tissue is differentiated as it is the main growing point. In sympodial orchids there are up to 5 meristems just below the apical meristem; these only come into operation if the main apical meristem is damaged. Either these latter or the main meristem can be used for propagation. They have to be transferred to a culture medium where they can be subdivided and an unlimited number of new plants raised.

Method

This section is based on work carried out on Cymbidium, the genus with which most success has been achieved. As basic material either the shoot of a new growth or of a back bulb is used and this shoot should be 8–10 cm (3⅛–4 in.) long. In a sterile room, on a sterile surface, the outer leaves are carefully removed until the first lateral meristematic zones become visible. These, as well as the others, are dissected out by a clean, sterilized scalpel and transferred to the growing medium. It is always advisable to sterilize the meristem portion by dipping, for about 10 seconds, in a 15 per cent ethyl alcohol. The apex of the growing point is then removed and transferred to the growing medium.

The Knudson III recipe for germinating orchid seeds is also ideal as a growing medium for tissue transplants. The receptacles and medium itself are prepared as described on p. 105. The test tubes or flasks should then be kept at 22 °C (c. 71 °F) and given about 12 hours of light per day. In the course of a few weeks the tissues turn green and grow into a protocorm. At its periphery the protocorm will grow rhizoids and later roots and leaves will develop. Often the protocorm will divide itself and by further subdivision a great number of growths appear. If the test tubes are mechanically rotated on a klinostat in order to counteract polarization leaves and shoots soon develop. For genera other than Cymbidium this is essential. The speed of rotation should be about two revolutions per minute. Once the plantlets have reached a size suitable for pricking out they are removed from the test tubes and planted out, the treatment being similar to that for seedlings. Success is only achieved if all the work is carried out in a sterile atmosphere.

The above description gives only a brief résumé of the method: much more complex apparatus is necessary to propagate other genera successfully. In Cattleya and its allies there is only about 50 per cent success even when the most careful and sophisticated techniques are used.

PESTS AND DISEASES

As with all other plants, orchids in the wild are subject to disease of various kinds as well as attacks by numerous pests. Many of these diseases are transmitted into the greenhouse by imported orchids, others are introduced from different sources. Healthy plants usually withstand infections and many a calamity can be prevented by high standards of cleanliness in cultivation.

To deal with all possible aspects of plant pathology one would need to write a comprehensive book on the subject. The following chapter, therefore, will only outline the most common pests and diseases that can be encountered in orchid cultivation. The beginner is advised to consult a specialist if faced by a serious outbreak of disease in his plant stock.

Fortunately it can be said that, in general, orchids are quite hardy and less liable than other indoor plants to catch diseases or attract pests. Moreover, the advent of modern chemicals allows us to control most infections efficiently or even prevent their occurence.

The development of commercial preparations is so rapid that brand names are often quickly out of date. For this reason only a few are given here. The reader should always seek the advice of an established dealer before using any pesticide. He should also be aware that the majority of these products are potentially dangerous to humans and pets and must therefore be used with care, especially when applied inside the home. (To the amateur and gardener alike the booklet on chemicals for the gardener (see bibliography p. 208) issued by H. M. Stationery Office is thoroughly recommended.)

Pests

Greenfly, although a fairly common pest in the greenhouse, is found only occasionally on orchids. They are easily recognizable because of their green colour and their quick movements. One will usually find them on young soft shoots and on buds and they may either be washed off or destroyed by fumigation; spraying has also been proved effective. Recommended for fumigation are a Murfume bomb or Fumite Lindane smoke pellets; for spraying, any proprietary product (such as Cooper's Garden spray) can be used.

Red Spider is not frequently found on orchids but if given favourable conditions it will settle on Dendrobium, Phalaenopsis and other soft-leaved orchids. Its presence can be recognized by the appearance of yellowish or white mottled patches on the leaves, which later may become bronzed. Hardly as big as a pinhead, it is usually of reddish colour. Its presence—mainly on the under surface of the leaf—is indicative of a dry atmosphere, thus properly cared for orchids should be fairly safe. If, however, plants have been attacked, immediate action should be taken. In the early stages of the infestation the leaves should simply be sponged with a nicotine solution; at later stages recommended insecticides must be sprayed. Since the insects produce thousands of tiny eggs, which rapidly produce a new generation, spraying has to be repeated at frequent intervals. In order to counteract the formation of resistant strains, an occasional change of insecticide is advisable.

Scale insects attack orchids frequently. Hard-leaved orchids such as Cattleya, Cymbidium, Bifrenaria, Lycaste, Odontoglossum, Oncidium, Vanda and others are especially liable to damage from scale insects. They are rather small and appear as tiny circular patches but can reach a diameter of almost 3 mm ($\frac{1}{8}$ in.) in the extreme. Whereas the nymphs are active, adults with their hardened scale remain stationary. Often sponging or brushing the affected leaves with soap and water will be sufficient. Severe infestations, however, must be tackled with potent insecticides such as Malathion.

Woolly aphid and mealy bug produce protective white woolly or waxy masses on stems and leaves. The repellent nature of this substance renders most sprays or powder insecticides ineffective. The best method is frequent sponging or brushing of the infested surfaces. In serious cases tar-based washes should be applied.

Thrips are minute yellowish-brown winged insects causing mottling of leaves and flowers. They deposit their eggs in the tissue of stems and leaves where the larvae develop, causing damage to the plant by sucking the juices. Thrips favour a hot dry atmosphere. Indicative of thrips infestation are glaucous patches or rusty spots on the leaves, distorted buds, and a blackish or whitish discoloration on the flowers. Odontoglossums, Miltonias and Paphiopedilums are particularly liable to

Pests

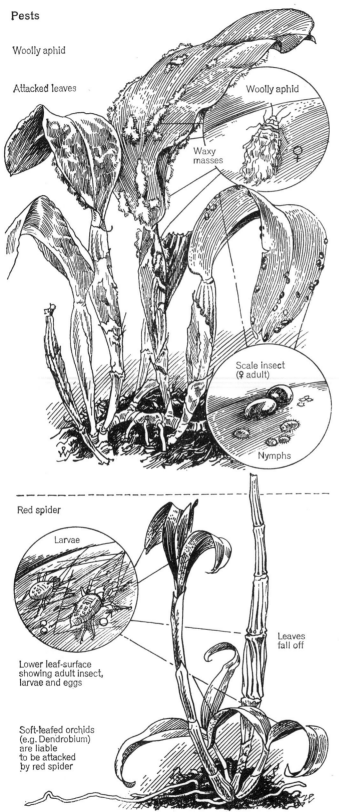

Woolly aphid

Attacked leaves

Woolly aphid

Waxy masses

Scale insect (♀ adult)

Nymphs

Red spider

Larvae

Lower leaf-surface showing adult insect, larvae and eggs

Leaves fall off

Soft-leafed orchids (e.g. Dendrobium) are liable to be attacked by red spider

thrips infestation but strictly speaking no single orchid is safe from their attack. The best remedy is spraying with Malathion at regular intervals of 2–3 months. As in other instances a change of preparation should be made from time to time otherwise the insects may become immune.

Cockroaches can cause great damage to root tips and they also attack Cattleya flowers. If not checked in time the damage may lead to a total loss of the plant. Prevention is better than cure and thus to eliminate all possible hiding places for these troublesome insects is the best solution. They usually shelter in dry warm places near heating pipes. One can easily trap them by using slightly hollowed potato-slices under which they assemble in numbers. Cooper's Pybuthrin powder has been recommended by various experts as a plant remedy. Besides this some arsenic-based commercial preparations can be applied.

Crickets, although less common in the greenhouse, can cause similar damage, but they can be checked in the same way.

Ants never attack orchids but they act as carriers of scale insects from one plant to another. Because of their peculiar living habits they cannot be destroyed as easily as other insects; sprays or even smokes are rarely effective. If chemicals fail one should attract them by

122

laying out baits such as bones, sweetened bread, meat or shallow saucers of oil. David Sander recommends fresh putty which attracts them. Treacle and arsenic is very effective but rather dangerous for general use in or near domestic dwellings.

Springtails are attractive minute wingless jumping insects living in the soil where they cause damage to young roots. They are easily controlled by a solution of nicotine and soap.

Slugs and, to a lesser extent, small snails are fond of root tips, young shoots, buds and certain orchid flowers. Because they are only active at night they are often not discovered before extensive damage has been done, but they can be collected at nightly inspections of the plant stock. Commercial preparations have to be viewed with some reservation since many of them only paralyse the animal for a short period. Recommended are metaldehyde mixtures. A tuft of cotton wool fixed on the stem beneath the inflorescence will prevent slugs and snails from reaching the flowers.

Diseases

Black rot. This is caused by the micro-organism *Pythium ultimum* and frequently occurs on Cattleya, Laeliocattleya, Laelia and a few other orchids. The disease usually

123

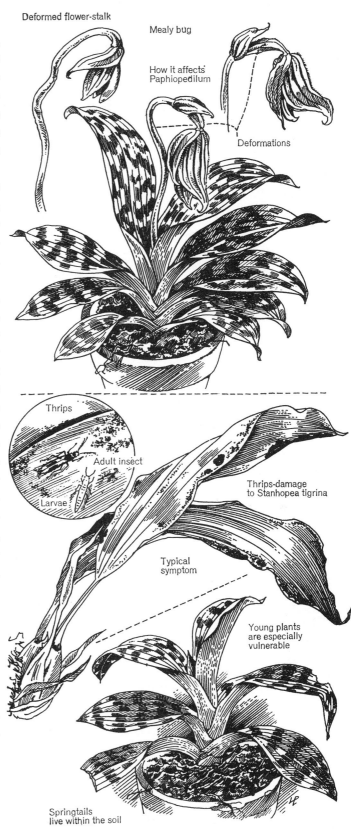

Deformed flower-stalk

Mealy bug

How it affects Paphiopedilum

Deformations

Thrips

Adult insect

Larvae

Thrips-damage to Stanhopea tigrina

Typical symptom

Young plants are especially vulnerable

Springtails live within the soil

Pests
(continued)

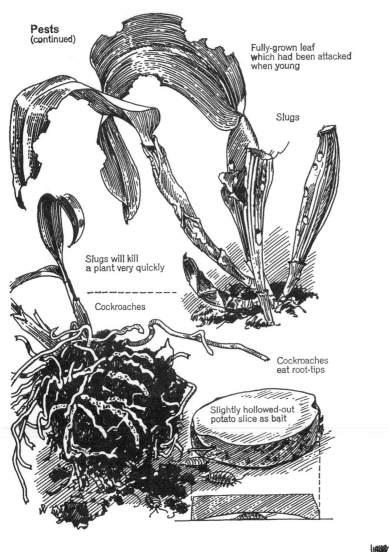

Fully-grown leaf
which had been attacked
when young

Slugs

Slugs will kill
a plant very quickly

Cockroaches

Cockroaches
eat root-tips

Slightly hollowed-out
potato slice as bait

Diseases

Black rot infested seedlings

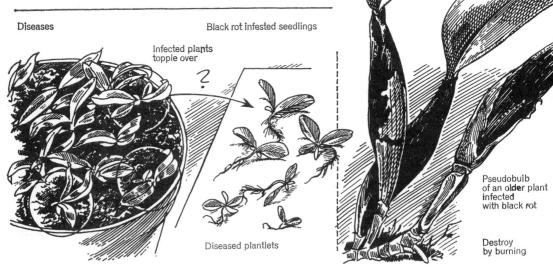

Infected plants
topple over

Diseased plantlets

Pseudobulb
of an older plant
infected
with black rot

Destroy
by burning

1 Paphiopedilum Dorama; **2** P. Renton × Bahram; **3** P. King Arthur 'Alexanderae'; **4** P. Weser

1 Miltonia flavescens; 2 Cattleya hybrid; 3 Odontioda hybrid; 4 Oncidium pusillum

1 Coelogyne ochracea; **2** Coelogyne cristata; **3** Odontoglossum cervantesii; **4** Odontoglossum humeanum; **5** Maxillaria punctata; **6** Cattleya loddigesii

1 Ansellia africana; 2 Calanthe triplicata (= C. veratrifolia); 3 Lycaste virginalis (= L. skinneri); 4 Brassia gireoudiana; 5 Sophrolaeliocattleya Psyche; 6 Stanhopea tigrina; 7 Masdevallia ignea; 8 Miltonia hybrids

starts in the roots, from where it spreads to the pseudobulbs which begin to shrivel. It may also appear first on the leaf-tips spreading quickly and causing a blackish discoloration. Pseudobulbs affected by black rot exhibit a yellowish or brownish discoloration in the shape of longitudinal streaks. The disease is highly infectious and spreads rapidly from plant to plant. Thus once black rot has been recognized the diseased part of the plant—or even the whole plant—should be cut-off and burnt. The healthy part of the plant must then be kept fairly dry and in well-aerated surroundings. Seedlings affected by black rot should be treated with a 1 : 100,000 solution of copper sulphate (see also Withner, p. 428).

Gleosporium leaf-spot is a disease which starts with minute but well-defined dark brown circular spots on the leaves. At a later stage these spots run together, forming large streaks, and finally the whole leaf turns reddish brown. If the infected leaves are not removed in time the fungus will spread to the pseudobulbs and thus destroy the entire plant. Diseased plants should be removed at once and treated with a copper-based fungicide at frequent intervals. The disease is mainly found on Cattleyas but may also occur on *Coelogyne cristata*, Laelia species and *Paphiopedilum philippinense*.

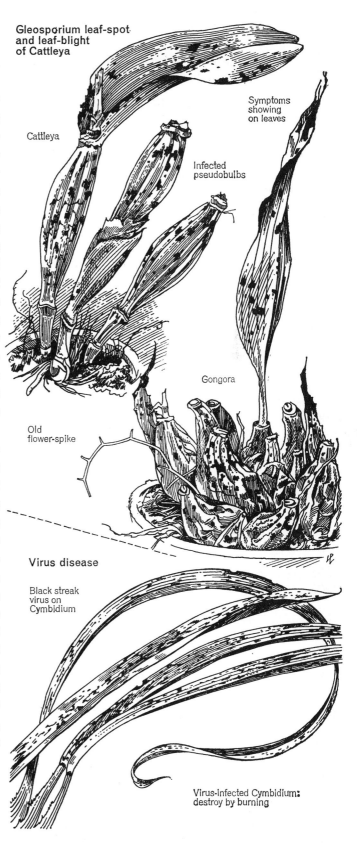

Gleosporium leaf-spot and leaf-blight of Cattleya

Cattleya

Symptoms showing on leaves

Infected pseudobulbs

Gongora

Old flower-spike

Virus disease

Black streak virus on Cymbidium

Virus-infected Cymbidium: destroy by burning

Leaf blight of Cattleya is caused by *Pythium splendens*. The infection becomes apparent by circular brown spots near the leaf margins. Later the entire leaf turns black. As high humidity favours this disease, increased ventilation combined with a reduction of the moisture content of the air is the best way of control. At the same time one should cut down on watering and infected parts of the plant must be burnt.

Damaging virus diseases are fortunately rare in orchids. Generally speaking our knowledge of virus infections, particularly of orchids, is still rather limited. The most common disease of this nature is the Black Streak Virus which is usually confined to Cymbidiums. Once a plant is badly infected by virus it cannot be cured and should therefore be destroyed. As always, prevention is better than cure. Make sure that you only acquire virus-free plants. Since the virus is spread by aphids, red spider and leaf-piercing insects make sure that these pests are eliminated. Moreover virus can be transmitted from one plant to another by knives or scissors. One should therefore never use the same tool for diseased and healthy plants. The usual routine cleansing of tools in detergent is not sufficient for removing the contaminant but dipping them into a copper sulphate solution should be effective.

THE BASIS OF ORCHID BREEDING—GENETICS

For the proper understanding of orchid breeding if you wish either to carry it out yourself or to observe the results of others (by perusing the monthly lists of new orchid hybrids, for example) a basic knowledge of genetics is desirable. It is a vast subject, touching on the disciplines of cytology, physiology, biochemistry, taxonomy, ecology and evolutionary studies.

Johann Gregor Mendel, an Abbot of Brno in what is now Czechoslovakia, in 1865 undertook crossing experiments on garden plants, mainly beans and peas. From these he deduced the 'Mendelian' laws of heredity. Basically he deduced the distribution of parental characters in their hybrid offspring.

There are two basic types of hereditable factors: those that are strongly manifested in the offspring are the 'dominant' characters and those that are passed on unnoticed are the 'recessives'.

Heredity means the handing down of the parents' characters to their offspring. These characters are not necessarily handed down evenly and offspring of a given set of parents may vary considerably. The reasons for this may be genetic or environmental.

The mechanism for handing on hereditary factors is located in the chromosomes of the nucleus of a plant's cells or, to be more precise, in the genes in the chromosomes. Each chromosome, itself microscopically small, carries an enormous number of genes. Generally speaking, all the individuals of a given species have the same number of chromosomes. Furthermore, but again generally speaking, all species of a genus have basically the same chromosome number.

Occasionally, however, individual plants of a species may have different chromosome numbers. Usually, in orchids, this is obvious from the differences in size and other factors between plants but sometimes there are no discernible differences. The fact that plants of the same species can have different chromosome numbers is of great importance horticulturally. It happens very often in those orchids most commonly grown and especially in those that have been in cultivation for a long period. For example, modern Paphiopedilum hybrids nearly all have double the

131

usual number of chromosomes and this is surely obvious in the substantial and luxuriant appearance of such plants.

Until recently, nearly all orchid breeding programmes were intuitively based and even today much breeding is carried out on an ad-hoc basis. The only guideline for the choice of parent plants was their appearance and perhaps their hardiness and flowering times. Sometimes successes were great but so were the failures. Attempted matings between apparently ideal parents often resulted in complete failure to produce any seed.

Today our increasing insight into genetical processes allows us to approach breeding on a really scientific and rational basis. The number of chromosomes is important if one is choosing likely parents for hybridization. Counting chromosomes which are only visible in dividing cell nuclei, is a tedious process and can only be carried on under a high-powered microscope. Cell division takes place continually at the growing points of roots and shoots and is called mitosis. There is another stage at which chromosomes may be observed and that is during the 'reduction division' in the production of gametes and this is termed meiosis. It can be observed in flowering buds in the earliest stages of development.

The basic chromosome number of a genus or species is called the haploid and is indicated as X. This number is actually only contained in a plant's gametes, the cells of a plant generally containing twice this number, i.e. 2X, or diploid as it is usually termed. If these numbers are multiplied they are referred to as polyploids. If these are high numbers they are usually expressed in the habit of the plant which is larger or maybe smaller.

The knowledge of a few genetic terms will be useful:

Diploid = 2X. Most plants and animals found in nature have two sets of chromosomes and are called diploids. Most orchid species in cultivation are diploids. The sexual behaviour of these plants follows the usual pattern and they set fertile seeds.

Tetraploid = 4X. By means both naturally and artificially induced, some plants have four sets of chromosomes and are called tetraploids. They are usually larger in all aspects, especially in their larger and showier flowers, and for this reason are ideal for exhibition and breeding. Most tetraploids are fertile and their cultivation poses no special problems.

Triploid = 3X. When a diploid is crossed with a tetraploid the resulting orchid is usually a triploid, i.e. it has three sets of chromosomes. These plants have a very low fertility rating but if crossed either with another triploid or a very vigorous diploid fertile seed may be produced. Thus triploids can be very important in breeding programmes and many of the modern hybrids are also in this category.

Pentaploid = 5X. Plants with this relatively high degree of polyploidy are rarely encountered. Because of their odd genetic make-up they are poor breeding partners but may nevertheless possess character excelling those of diploids or tetraploids.

Octoploids = 8X. Recently some orchid hybrids with eight sets of chromosome numbers have been produced. As well as exhibiting unique floral features, they also have different flowering times which is of great commercial significance.

Aneuploids. Plants with incomplete sets of chromosomes are called aneuploids. The quality of such plants is variable as is their breeding behaviour. If used as parents the results may be dismal failures or great successes.

Breeding

The fascinating history of orchid breeding from the time the first artificial hybrid was flowered by John Dominy in 1856 until 1960 when the Royal Horticultural Society took over the responsibility of maintaining the 'stud' books from the famed orchid house of Sander, has been dealt with in considerable detail in my earlier book, *The Orchid World.* To bring the story up-to-date the International Registration

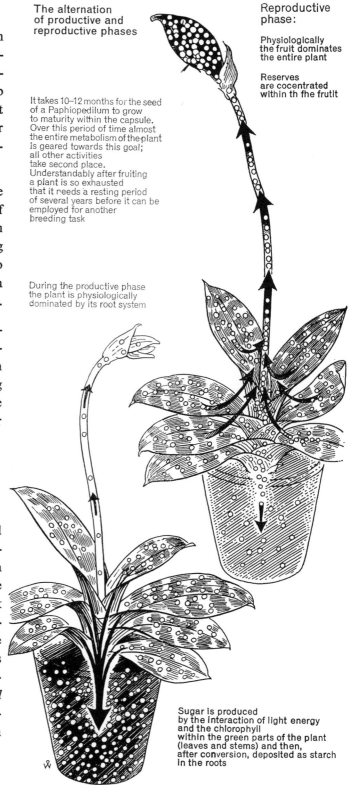

The alternation of productive and reproductive phases

Reproductive phase:

Physiologically the fruit dominates the entire plant

Reserves are cocentrated within th fhe frutit

It takes 10–12 months for the seed of a Paphiopedilum to grow to maturity within the capsule. Over this period of time almost the entire metabolism of the plant is geared towards this goal; all other activities take second place. Understandably after fruiting a plant is so exhausted that it needs a resting period of several years before it can be employed for another breeding task

During the productive phase the plant is physiologically dominated by its root system

Sugar is produced by the interaction of light energy and the chlorophyll within the green parts of the plant (leaves and stems) and then, after conversion, deposited as starch in the roots

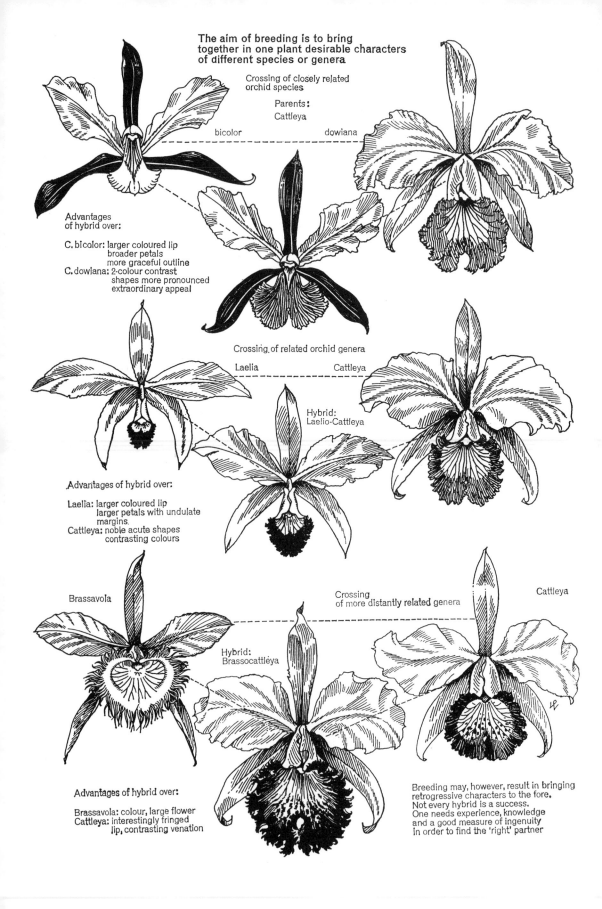

The aim of breeding is to bring
together in one plant desirable characters
of different species or genera

Crossing of closely related
orchid species

Parents:
Cattleya

bicolor   dowiana

Advantages
of hybrid over:

C. bicolor: larger coloured lip
broader petals
more graceful outline
C. dowiana: 2-colour contrast
shapes more pronounced
extraordinary appeal

Crossing of related orchid genera

Laelia   Cattleya

Hybrid:
Laelio-Cattleya

Advantages of hybrid over:

Laelia: larger coloured lip
larger petals with undulate
margins.
Cattleya: noble acute shapes
contrasting colours

Brassavola   Cattleya

Crossing
of more distantly related genera

Hybrid:
Brassocattleya

Advantages of hybrid over:

Brassavola: colour, large flower
Cattleya: interestingly fringed
lip, contrasting venation

Breeding may, however, result in bringing
retrogressive characters to the fore.
Not every hybrid is a success.
One needs experience, knowledge
and a good measure of ingenuity
in order to find the 'right' partner

Authority for orchid hybrids at the RHS, together with the International Orchid Commission on Classification, Nomenclature and Registration, has produced a Handbook on Orchid Nomenclature and Registration which sets out the rules necessary for naming and registering new hybrids.

For the amateur enthusiast the decision to start a breeding programme is a weighty one. The parent plant itself has first to be considered. The bearing of a capsule will not only interrupt the normal life cycle of the plant but, as the capsule takes such a long time to reach maturity it may take much sustenance and vitality from the parent. Second, since so very many seeds will be produced and since each one could possibly contain the embryo of a world champion the enthusiast will have to reconcile himself to the fact that it will not be possible to germinate all the seeds, nor, furthermore, will it be possible to raise all the seedlings to flowering size. The contents of a single capsule, if all were germinated and grown-on, would fill several 100-foot greenhouses. The breeder of orchids also needs very considerable patience, since the time taken from the cross-pollinating of the parents to the flowering of the resulting offspring is usually several years and at least five. However, with such a wide variety of orchids

135

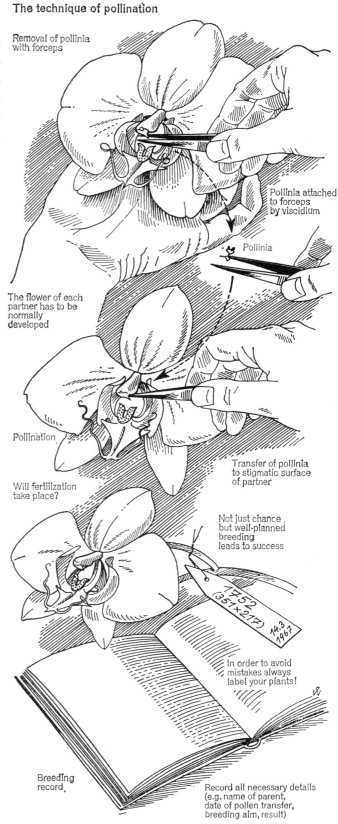

Removal of pollinia with forceps

Pollinia attached to forceps by viscidium

Pollinia

The flower of each partner has to be normally developed

Pollination

Transfer of pollinia to stigmatic surface of partner

Will fertilization take place?

Not just chance but well-planned breeding leads to success

In order to avoid mistakes always label your plants!

Breeding record

Record all necessary details (e.g. name of parent, date of pollen transfer, breeding aim, result)

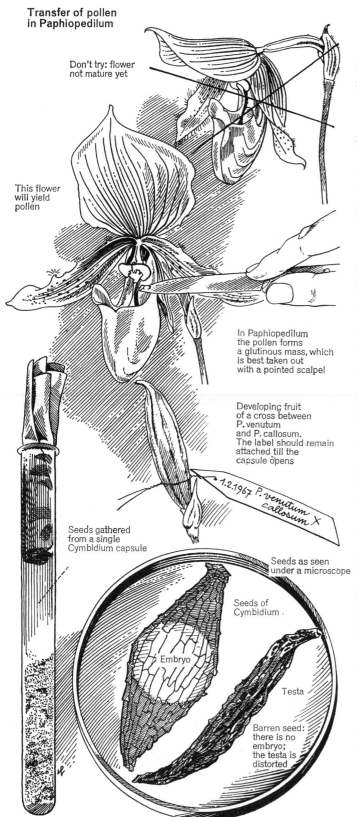

**Transfer of pollen
in Paphiopedilum**

Don't try: flower
not mature yet

This flower
will yield
pollen

In Paphiopedilum
the pollen forms
a glutinous mass, which
is best taken out
with a pointed scalpel

Developing fruit
of a cross between
P. venutum
and P. callosum.
The label should remain
attached till the
capsule opens

1.2.1967 P. venutum
callosum ×

Seeds gathered
from a single
Cymbidium capsule

Seeds as seen
under a microscope

Seeds of
Cymbidium .

Embryo

Testa

Barren seed:
there is no
embryo;
the testa is
distorted

available as potential parents the newest amateur orchid breeder may indeed produce many new hybrids worthy of international acclaim.

In earlier times, but not counting the earliest pioneer days, most breeding was aimed at producing more and better flowers for commercial reasons. Today, however, many amateurs, and the more adventurous commercial growers, frequently experiment in their hybridization programmes and many interesting and unusual new plants have been produced.

Because of their considerable promiscuity, orchids not only hybridize freely within the same genus but between species of related genera and furthermore, the offspring from these are usually just as fertile. Today hybrid genera are known with two, three, four and even five genera entering into their constitution. Over 230 hybrid genera have been so far recorded and the list grows monthly.

As far as the naming of these new genera are concerned, if only two genera are involved the new name is a combination of the parents' names either wholly or partially e.g. Brassocattleya (Brassavola × Cattleya). Laeliocattleya (Laelia × Cattleya); if three genera are involved the new name can either be formed in the same manner as for two genera, e.g. Brassolaeliocattleya, or a new name can be

136

1 Gomesa crispa; 2 Sobralia macrantha; 3 Dendrobium phalaenopsis;
4 Paphiopedilum glaucophyllum; 5 Vanda teres; 6 Huntleya burtii;
7 Vanda burgeffii; 8 Disa uniflora; 9 Bulbophyllum falcatum

1 Fruit of a Cattleya; 2 Cattleya seedlings in the test tube; 3 Cattleya seedlings in successive stages of growth; 4 Paphiopedilum, young plants in successive stages of development; 5 Paphiopedilum seedlings in their first community pot; 6 Cattleya seedlings in second community pot

coined based on the name of some person or place prominent in orchid breeding, growing, or botany, with the termination -ara e.g. Hawaiiara (Vanda × Renanthera × Vandopsis); in the case of four genera being involved a new name ending in -ara must always be used e.g. Potinara (Brassavola × Cattleya × Laelia × Sophronitis).

Purist orchid growers often have a natural aversion to orchid hybrids, preferring the unmolested products of nature. In support of their views perhaps the first priority of all orchid growers should be to cultivate and propagate those species which are in danger of extinction in the wild either from habitat destruction or over-collection. Nevertheless breeding programmes can produce plants that are a great improvement on those found growing wild and they bring to the surface the genetic potentialities inherent in wild species. Such characters include shape, size, colour, flowering time, flower productivity and longevity. For example, the combination of Cochlioda species with various Odontoglossums gives a range of Odontiodas with colour nuances far superior to any shown by the untouched species.

Perhaps equally important, especially commercially, is that hybridization makes it possible to have orchids flowering at any time of the year in unlimited quantities.

Orchid breeding has had a glorious past, is thriving at present and has an exciting future.

Method

The physical transference of pollinia from the male to the stigmatic surface of the female is simple but to achieve fertilization is a different matter. Only orchids that are genetically related can be crossed: it is not possible, for example, to fertilize successfully a Paphiopedilum with a Vanda or a Cattleya.

It was once essential that the potential parents should be flowering at the same time and in the same place. However, with the advent of two relatively recent technological breakthroughs these 'essentials' are no longer paramount. The greatly increased speeds of air transport mean that the flowers, or at least their pollinia, can be flown in the viable state from one corner of the world to the other and this greatly increases the possibilities of crossing. Second, it has been proved possible to store pollinia under certain conditions, such as drying or freezing and for them to remain usable and capable of fertilizing several months after the flower from which they were removed has died.

Pollination should take place as soon as possible after the flower from which the pollinia are taken is mature. The special structure of the orchid flower has been shown on pp. 12–15. The pollinia, situated at the top of the column, can easily be detached with forceps or even with a sliver of wood. They are then transferred to the sticky stigmatic surface of the female parent where they adhere immediately. In the case of Paphiopedilum it is advisable to remove the pouch-shaped labellum before pollinating as it somewhat obscures the stigma. Pollination does not, of course, equal fertilization. A considerable period, up to several months, may elapse between pollination and the actual process of fertilization (as was explained on p. 15). After pollination both parent flowers start to wither and wilt. A swelling of the ovary does not always spell success and it is so very disappointing to see, expectantly after pollination, the capsule quickly swell but then slowly turn yellow and eventually fall, infertile, to the ground. However, even an apparently normal capsule, just before dehiscence, may contain sterile seed, if any at all. To determine whether a seed is usable or not it should be examined under the microscope. In fertile seeds, upon microscopic examination the embryo is very obvious. With sterile seeds the embryo is badly shrivelled. The presence of any embryo, however, is no guarantee. The viability of seed is about six months under normal conditions but when stored under low pressure, temperature and humidity their life-span is greatly increased.

MONTH BY MONTH IN YOUR ORCHID HOUSE

In temperate parts of the world to ensure successful continued growth and flowering of orchid collections it is necessary to carry out a yearly routine of cultural operations. The suggested monthly tasks are given below, but it must always be borne in mind that conditions vary from locality to locality and account must be taken of yearly climatic changes. Of prime importance in applying these routine operations is the condition of the plants. The tyro strives to learn and establish basic foolproof rules but these cannot be given. As mentioned before, it is always possible that if the opposite of the rules is applied success, perversely, can be achieved but one should not be blinded by short-term successes for orchids are plants of marked longevity. The rhythm of plant life is governed in temperate regions by the more or less regular periodicity of the seasons.

The resting period is a factor of great importance. The most crucial period in an orchid's history is basically the months February to April when it is just starting to grow, this is followed by the period of most active growth lasting from May to July, and the third season to note is the maturing phase from August to September. In October the growth period comes to an end and the plant prepares itself for the minor resting period from November to January. This is only a rough guide and each plant has its own method of growth which only experience will elucidate.

All operations are conditioned by plant growth in relation to the season. The temperatures should be as follows (variations of 2–3° are tolerable over short periods):

	day	night
c:	13°C (55°F)	10°C (50° F)
i:	16–18°C (61–65° F)	15–16°C (59–61°F)
w:	21°C (70°F)	19–21°C (66–70°F)

Even if plants are cultivated in the greenhouse the temperature can be influenced by outside conditions such as rainfall or wind. Significant drops in temperature may also occur on cloudless nights. If there are prolonged periods of dull cold weather, humidity within the greenhouse should be controlled carefully. Whatever the temperature, there should never be an excessive amount of humidity. Water only in the morning. If you spray or damp down in the afternoon make sure that there is sufficient heat to allow the plant surfaces to dry up before the onset of night. The lower the temperature, the less moisture should be allowed for orchids which have to be left cool.

Cattleya/Laelia: Temperatures moderate to prevent premature shoots (16–18°C [61–65°F] in daytime; 12–15°C [54–59°F] at night). The potting material should never be allowed to dry out. Keep plants in bud a little more moist than others.

Cymbidium: Moderately moist but not wet. Plants in bud should be kept fairly moist but not warm, otherwise the buds may turn yellow and fall off. Resting plants should be left in a humid atmosphere.

Paphiopedilum: Reduce moisture only slightly. Temperature as indicated above but slightly higher for plants with developing buds.

Phalaenopsis: Evenly high temperature, no resting period. Do not allow the potting material to dry out as this will endanger the plant. The bud development requires strong light in order to prevent yellowing.

Dendrobium: Strict resting period whatever the temperature requirements. Temperature according to origin of plant. Moisture moderate to low; make sure of sufficient humidity. Beware of red spider and thrips (see pp. 120–123).

Hard bulbed plants such as Oncidium, Odontoglossum and similar ones need hardly any water.

Deciduous orchids, such as Calanthe, Catasetum, etc., are to be kept completely dry.

Paphiopedilums of the warmer kind, provided they are not in bud or flower, can be repotted. Afterwards keep moisture to a limit but spray or damp down frequently.

In favourable conditions new roots will have developed towards the end of the month; the most difficult time for the plant has come to an end.

February

Should wintery weather still prevail, impose a similar régime as prescribed for January. There may, however, be more rapid temperature changes. Increased intensity of the sun may already influence the temperature of plants grown under glass, on the other hand any drop of temperature at night can be more severe. Therefore make sure that your thermostat is functioning properly. If a lowering of temperature cannot be avoided it should be accompanied by a decrease in humidity. Plants cultivated in the living room are under great stress because the domestic heating system keeps the room rather dry. It might help to cover the plants with cellophane or other transparent foil. Additional lighting is essential and should be supplied from dusk to about 22.00 hrs. An even longer period of artificial lighting is required on dull days. Without the help of additional lighting bud-formation will be delayed, if not prevented. Towards the end of the month sunny days may already necessitate some shading, especially for Phalaenopsis and Paphiopedilum.

Cattleya/Laelia: With the exception of flowering or budding specimens the plants are still at rest. Towards the end of the month humidity should be increased on sunny days.

Cymbidium: Plants in bud or flower require a fair amount of moisture. Keep the temperature relatively low by means of ventilation. Beware of bumble bees which may enter the greenhouse; if they enter the flowers they will destroy them by taking the pollinia. Plants not in flower should be kept cool and moderately moist.

Paphiopedilum: If the plants have no buds repotting must now take place. Avoid excessive soil moisture as well as drying out. Spray early in the day but allow the plant surfaces to be dry in the evening.

Phalaenopsis: An even amount of moisture and sufficient light are of paramount importance for proper bud-development. During prolonged spells of dull weather they easily turn yellow and fall off.

Dendrobium: Species of the cool section remain in cool and relatively dry conditions; *D. nobile* and its forms and varieties may show first buds. Species of the warmer section also remain at rest and should be kept at 15–18°C (59–65°F) and not too moist.

143

Odontoglossum, Oncidium and related genera are still resting. *Odontoglossum grande* should never be sprayed but the potting medium requires some water.

Vanda: *V. coerulea, V. bicolor* and their allies require plenty of light, moderate warmth and not much water during their resting period. Species and hybrids of the warmer section such as *V. sanderana* should be kept constantly moist, and all through the winter they require two hours or more of additional artificial light per day in order to secure flowering.

March

In marked contrast to February the onset of the vegetative period makes itself felt more powerfully. Shoot development sets in but can either be delayed or encouraged. It is favoured by increased moisture and humidity as well as by increased temperature and light. On the other hand the resting period can be artificially extended by low temperature and lack of moisture. In any case both extremes should be avoided in order not to interfere too much with the inherent growing rhythm of each individual species.

Sudden large changes in temperature are no longer to be feared. The sun intensity increases rapidly and thus relieves the internal heating system. Nevertheless it is often rather difficult to control the temperature at the beginning of the month, especially when the outside temperature drops at night. On sunny days greenhouse plants or plants in large plant windows facing south require a fair measure of shading. One should always bear in mind that after all the dark months the plants have gradually to adapt themselves to this abundance of light. If exposed to it suddenly, damage may ensue.

Moisture should be increased only gradually. Spraying and damping should take precedence over watering. Too much moisture in the soil is detrimental to root development. As a rule the plants should not be watered after midday, especially when cool nights are to be expected. Plants of all temperature sections may now be repotted.

	day	night
c:	13–16°C (55–61°F)	10–12°C (50–54°F)
i:	18–21°C (65–70°F)	16–18°C (61–65°F)
w:	21–23°C (70–73°F)	c. 21°C (70°F)

Cattleya/Laelia: The relatively large leaf-surfaces of these plants are liable to overheat if exposed to sunlight. If they feel warm to the touch shade and/or increase ventilation. Note that the temperature of the leaf is not the same as the temperature

144

of the surrounding air. The correlation of these factors, although of great importance to the well-being of plants, is still not properly understood.

Cymbidium: Plants that have finished flowering or non-flowering specimens should be offered a maximum of light, a generous degree of humidity but also a good measure of fresh air. Repotting should only take place if essential since great care must be taken of the fleshy roots. Cymbidiums often react to repotting by not flowering in the following season.

Paphiopedilum: Allow for high humidity and well observed shading as this will favour the formation of new roots.

Phalaenopsis: High temperature and humidity in connection with some shading will be beneficial to root- and leaf-development. Phalaenopsis should be repotted annually but this can be done until well into August if conditions are favourable.

Dendrobium: Species originating from the Indo-Malayan monsoon regions are now in flower.

Dendrobium phalaenopsis, including its forms and hybrids, should be repotted now or next month. If repotting has taken place the temperature must be kept fairly high. Newly formed shoots are rather sensitive to spraying, make sure that they are dry over night otherwise they will rot.

Odontoglossum and **Oncidium** are now repotted. One should avoid excessive heat and moisture but they need as much light as possible.

Calanthe: The pseudobulbs of species and hybrids of the deciduous section, which have been at rest so far, show new root-development. They are to be repotted. Make sure that they get high temperatures and plenty of light; moisture should be increased gradually.

Coelogyne: If necessary all species are now repotted and reshaped.

April

In this month both growth and root-formation become more rigorous. With the higher position of the sun, light and temperatures will rise accordingly. Therefore special attention should be paid to shading. Whereas the moisture in the potting material must be kept moderate humidity should be increased. In order to cope with sudden changes in the outside temperature make sure that your heating equipment is still at the ready.

Temperatures may be as follows:

145

day	night
c: 16–18°C (61–65°F)	c. 13°C (55°F)
i: 18–21°C (65–70°F)	16–18°C (61–65°F)
w: 21–23°C (70–73°F)	c. 21°C (70°F)

Cattleya: Repotting is continued, but should come to an end towards the end of the month to allow for healthy shoot-development. The only exceptions are the still resting species and hybrids of *Cattleya gaskelliana, C. warscewiczii, C. schroederae,* provided they are not in bud. Very often it proves difficult to hold back precocious shoots which will jeopardize flowering. Too much light makes the plants turn yellowish, therefore moderate shading should be applied.

Cymbidium: Plants which did not have to be repotted are transferred to the cooler section of the house but they should receive plenty of fresh air. Freshly repotted specimens are carefully watered and best kept in a humid atmosphere.

Dendrobium: As recommended for March. Repotting can still be undertaken. Spray only before noon and keep plant surfaces dry overnight.

Block cultivation: The resting period for all miniatures is now over. If necessary they are either replanted or the growing medium is replenished. They need special attention; frequent spraying is recommended.

May

This is the first month of the summer, and one is less liable to make serious mistakes than during the resting period. Only species of the temperate and hot sections need heating. If the outside temperature is favourable air can be admitted to both the cool and the temperate house. In the second half of the month more hardy plants such as Coelogyne, Bifrenaria, *Odontoglossum grande,* Stanhopea, *Vanda tricolor* and others of this kind, may be transferred to the balcony or to sheltered positions in the garden. Also small greenhouses without heating can now be occupied, but all depends upon local climatic conditions. Thus, under certain circumstances, these operations may even take place towards the end of April or in the early days of May. One should still make provision for sudden temperature changes. At any rate all plants should only gradually be exposed to the abundance of light: shading must be provided at first otherwise the leaves may become overheated or even burnt. Temperatures should be as follows:

day	night
c: 16°C (61°F)	13–16°C (55–61°F)
i: 21–27°C (70–81°F)	18–21°C (65–70°F)
w: up to 32°C (90°F)	21–24°C (70–75°F)

Cattleya/Laelia: On sunny days spray 2–3 times a day. Fully grown plants should receive as much fresh air as possible. A suitably humid atmosphere can be created by damping the central gangway as well as all surfaces of the greenhouse. Laelia species, at least the robust ones, are kept a little harder than Cattleyas: they should receive more light and air but less heat.

Cymbidiums prefer a cool root ball, plenty of air, an even amount of moisture and a little shade. During the warm season they are best placed in the shade of trees but some sort of protection against sudden or prolonged rain must be provided (glass panes).

Paphiopedilum: Hardly any other orchid genus has such strongly differentiated temperature requirements. Species of all three temperature sections must be treated according to their section otherwise damage may occur. All species, however, need plenty of shade throughout the summer or even until October. *P. insigne* may be kept in a frame, perhaps together with *Coelogyne cristata* and Cymbidium.

Phalaenopsis: Good growth is guaranted by high temperature and humidity assisted by regular doses of feeds.

Dendrobium: Plants of the warm section such as *D. phalaenopsis*, *D. superbiens*, *D. bigibbum* are to be kept warm, bright and evenly moist. All the species originating from the Asian mainland must be kept moist and warm but given a good measure of fresh air. Weekly or fortnightly doses of manure (see also pp. 77–79) are recommended.

June-July

In these two months plant growth reaches its climax. All repotting operations are over except for summer-flowering Cattleyas which have to be repotted immediately after the flowers have gone. The daily routine must be strictly adhered to. Only young plants and exceptionally delicate species require additional heating. If a warm period is suddenly followed by a spell of cool and wet weather, watering and spraying must be undertaken carefully. Permanent shading devices should be temporarily removed in such circumstances. Well grown plants may now be manured provided that their root-system is fully developed.

On extremely warm days one may encounter difficulties in keeping down the temperature for orchids of the cool section. Frequent spraying is a possibility but it may lead to an over-saturation of the moisture in the potting material. The best course to take for plants of this group (e.g. *Odontoglossum crispum* and its hybrids, Cymbidium, *Odontoglossum grande*, Masdevallia) is to provide good shading in conjunction with proper ventilation.

147

Cattleya: In early developed specimens the new annual shoot may be fully mature by the end of July. If the flowers are expected soon it is impossible to allow the plant to rest at this stage. Thus the formation of yet another shoot must be accepted; alas it may not mature into the flowering stage.

Paphiopedilum: Sufficient shade is of great importance (see also May). A humid atmosphere can be guaranteed by damping all possible surfaces of the greenhouse.

Cymbidium: There should be enough ventilation to make the foliage of the plants quiver constantly.

Calanthe: For good formation of pseudobulbs high temperatures, plenty of moisture and liquid manuring are essential.

August

The beginning of this month is usually not much different from the second half of July but as the days grow shorter and the nights become cooler some changes make themselves felt. Most plants are by now fully matured or in the process of maturing. The observant gardener will assist his plants in this process as much as he possibly can. Since the temperatures are still relatively high at the beginning of the month moisture must be supplied freely, either by watering or by spraying. As the annual shoots mature water is gradually reduced. Shading appliances must be removed, especially in the morning and afternoon, when plenty of light must be available. Ventilation has still to be operated generously. Plants of the warm section as well as young plants already require additional heating; nightly precipitation can be dangerous for them.

Cattleya: If shade is reduced suddenly the plants may turn yellow. This sort of damage can hardly be remedied. Plants in flower must be protected against night dew otherwise the flowers will become speckled.

Miltonia: Repotting may take place now if not done in spring.

Odontoglossum: For *O. crispum* and its hybrids the end of August and the beginning of September is the best time for repotting but it can be continued till October.

Vanda: Fully grown plants should gradually be adapted to more light until they can be exposed to full sunlight. This will further the formation of buds.

September

Climatic changes make themselves felt much stronger than in the previous month. The days are now markedly shorter; therefore bud formation starts in many species. In order to delay this, additional lighting will be necessary in the morning and after sunset. Plants of the temperate section may be left without heating until the night temperature sinks below 15°C (59°F). The warm section must be heated now. The recommended temperatures for all three sections are given below:

	day	night
c:	15–18°C (59–65°F)	12–13°C (54–55°F)
i:	21–23°C (70–73°F)	15–18°C (59–65°F)
w:	up to 26°C (79°F)	21°C (70°F) or more

Special attention should be paid to the removal of shading devices in order to afford the plants maximum daylight. Never forget, however, that even now extremely warm days may occur; thus your arrangement should be flexible. Watering and spraying should be done carefully: plant surfaces should be dry at night; the moisture of the root-ball should be moderate. Under no circumstances should one keep the soil too dry at this stage. Plants which were positioned in the open during summer must be brought under cover by the middle of the month or even earlier if bad weather sets in. As in all other situations use your common sense.

Cattleya/Laelia: According to the state of shoot-development the plants should be kept more or less moist. If the annual shoot is still developing keep the root ball evenly moist.

Cymbidium: In order to encourage bud formation keep the temperature down, at night it should not go above 13°C (55°F). Cymbidium species are rather sensitive to excessive moisture; make sure that all plant surfaces are free from water.

Paphiopedilum: *P. insigne* must now be kept at about 13°C (55°F), especially overnight, in order to set flowers. Species and hybrids of the temperate section should be kept somewhat cooler for a period of 2–3 weeks as this will encourage bud development.

Dendrobium: The annual shoot will be matured in plants of both sections. For *D. nobile* and related species the resting period begins. *D. phalaenopsis* and its hybrids already show buds; in order to secure flowering additional lighting is recommended. Make sure that the flowers are kept dry!

Block cultivation: Miniatures without pseudobulbs have to be kept moist. A marked resting period would be detrimental to their survival since they have no organs for the preservation of water.

149

October

The humidity of the greenhouse or, for that matter of any place indoors, is relatively dependent on the humidity of the air outside. Therefore damping has now to be decreased accordingly. If, however, heating has to be increased because of falling outside temperatures it will result in a loss of humidity which must then be compensated by more damping. Watering should be gradually decreased. Make sure that none of the changes is effected rapidly. Shading has now become unnecessary. Clean all windows and glass panes in order to admit an optimum of light. On mild days allow for plenty of fresh air but avoid draughts. The recommended temperatures are as follows:

	day	night
c:	16°C (61°F)	12–13°C (54–55°F)
i:	18–21°C (65–70°F)	16–18°C (61–65°F)
w:	24°C (75°F)	21°C (70°F)

Cattleya: Plants with visible buds are kept moist. For those species that flower in winter or spring the resting period begins provided their annual shoot is fully matured: reduce water gradually and make sure that the pseudobulbs do not shrivel. Should a second new shoot break through within the following weeks, either cut it off or let it grow. In the latter case it will depress bud development.

Laelia: Plants which so far have been treated in the same way as Cattleyas may be kept cooler during their resting period and allowed more fresh air.

Cymbidium: They remain cool and well ventilated, and their root ball is kept evenly but moderately moist: stagnant moisture will result in the loss of roots.

Paphiopedilum: In order to guarantee perfect flowers keep the root ball constantly moist and create sufficient humidity. Lack of proper care during the following months may lead to an attack by red spider.

Odontoglossum: *O. grande* should not be sprayed any longer, but watered occasionally. When buds appear increase humidity slightly. *O. crispum* and its relatives demand a cool-damp atmosphere and temperatures about 12°C (54°F). The root ball is to be kept moist. *O. citrosmum* must be kept dry after the annual shoot has matured; otherwise it will not flower.

Dendrobium: *D. nobile* and related species are at rest; keep them cool and dry. *D. phalaenopsis* is still in flower; after flowering the resting period starts; keep the plants moderately moist at temperatures between 15–18°C (59–65°F).

Miltonia: These plants should, more or less, be kept as indicated for Cattleyas. Temperatures should be a fraction higher than in summer.

Calanthe: The leaves begin to die down. As buds develop and grow, water moderately until the flowers are wilted. Then keep the pseudobulbs absolutely dry.

November–December

During these darkest months of the year young plants as well as plants in bud require additional lighting (see also the chapter on lighting on pp. 65–69). On dull or misty days keep humidity down; make sure that fog does not enter the greenhouse. Mild sunny days may nevertheless require spraying before noon. High temperatures in the warm section may necessitate spraying twice daily. The temperatures should be as follows:

	day	night
c:	15°C (59°F)	13° (55°F)
i:	16–18°C (61–65°F)	16° (61°F)
w:	21–23°C (70–73°F)	21°C (70°F)

These figures may be a fraction lower on extremely cold days. At any rate avoid overheating. Special attention should be paid to possible attacks of pests since the warm atmosphere encourages their spread (see also p. 120). As the year draws to a close you will have time for reflecting on success or failure over the past season.

CULTIVATED ORCHIDS—AN ANNOTATED LIST

Since the first discovery of orchids, attempts have been made over the years to cultivate plants of species of nearly all the 750 genera now recognized. Many have been found not cultivatable and these include the saprophytes and many other terrestrials. However, perhaps all epiphytic genera have been grown at some time and today about 300 genera are widely represented in greenhouse collections. In choosing what to include and what to omit in the following selection note has been made of plants recently offered in nurserymen's catalogues or seen at shows. The generic and specific names used are usually those currently accepted as botanically correct: if there is more than one opinion equally held by competent botanists, that held at Kew is given. In some cases neither the generic nor specific name is correct but an incorrect or not currently accepted name is used instead, because to refer to the species by any other name would be confusing to growers and would upset the lists of orchid hybrids. Such 'incorrect' names are termed 'Horticultural Equivalents' or 'Recommended Names' and the rules governing them, together with a cross-referenced list, are given in the *Handbook on Orchid Nomenclature and Registration* (see p. 206).

Under each genus a note is given on whether the species should be grown as an epiphyte or terrestrial; on the approximate number of species so far recorded and their generalized distribution (N.B. 'tropical' includes 'subtropical'); on general cultivation and general description. Following this a note is made of the species more commonly cultivated and their distribution, and other particularly distinctive features are mentioned. A note is also made of the ease of cultivation of each species: I = beginners' orchids and those probably suitable for window sill cultivation, II = fairly easy species but requiring at least the controlled conditions of an indoor mini-greenhouse or plant-window, III = the most difficult subjects for which a well-equipped greenhouse is necessary.

The letters A–F indicate the type of potting medium to be used.

A: 3 parts osmunda, 1 part sphagnum, 1 part peat, 1 part grit
B: 2 parts osmunda, 2 parts sphagnum, 1 part peat, 1 part grit
C: 2 parts osmunda, 2 parts sphagnum
D: 2 parts chopped osmunda, 2 parts sphagnum, 2 parts grit, 2 parts peat, charcoal and bone meal added
E: 4 parts fibrous loam, 1 part sand, 1 part leafmould and/or chopped sphagnum
F: 2 parts osmunda, 1 part chopped sphagnum, 3 parts grit, 1 part charcoal

Acampe

Epiphytic; 15 species, tropical Africa, Madagascar, and tropical Asia. Warm or intermediate house with no definite resting period; compost F. Monopodial with fairly short stems, strap-shaped leaves and clusters of small yellowish flowers often marked reddish.

A. pachyglossa (Africa), III.

A. longifolia (India), II.

Acanthephippium

Terrestrial; 30 species, tropical Asia and Pacific Islands. Warm or intermediate house with a short resting period; compost B + 2 parts fibrous loam. Pseudobulbous with large leaves and short inflorescences bearing a few large dull yellow orange or pinkish flowers.

A. javanicum (Malaysia, Indonesia), III.

A. striatum (India, Java), III.

Acineta

Epiphytic; 15 species, tropical America. Warm or intermediate house with no marked resting period; compost A, preferably in a hanging basket. Pseudobulbous

153

with large leaves and long pendulous racemes of large, fleshy, fragrant flowers borne at the base.

A. chrysantha (Central America), III, bright yellow, spotted red flowers borne on 1 m. inflorescences.

A. densa (Costa Rica), III, colour as *A. chrysantha.*

A. superba (South America), II, pink petals, dull sepals, yellow lip.

Ada

Epiphytic; 2 species, Colombia. Cool house, keep slightly drier in winter; compost C. Pseudobulbous with spikes bearing many vermilion red flowers.

A. aurantiaca (Colombia), II, unspotted flowers.

A. aurantiaca punctata (Colombia), II, brown spotted flowers.

Aërangis

Epiphytic; 80 species, tropical Africa and Madagascar. Warm house with adequate moisture at all times; compost F. Monopodial with short stems, strap shaped or ovate leaves, pendulous spikes of star-like flowers up to 3 cm (1½ in.) across, usually white, with long spurs.

A. biloba (West Africa), III.

A. citrata (Madagascar), III, small, palest powder yellow fragrant flowers borne in profusion on long spikes.

A. kotschyana (East Africa), III, extra long salmon pink spurs.

A. rhodosticta (tropical Africa), III, flat, creamy-white flowers with brilliant red tipped column.

Aëranthes

Epiphytic; 30 species, Madagascar. Warm house with adequate moisture at all times; compost F. Monopodial with short stems, long leaves and pale, complex flowers usually borne singly at end of very long, very thin, delicate flower stems.

A. arachnites, III, green tepals, white lip.

A. grandiflora, III, bright green flowers.

A. henricii, III, extra large white flowers.

Aërides

Epiphytic; 40 species, tropical Asia. Warm or intermediate house with sufficient water at all times; compost F. Monopodial with usually very long stems, large

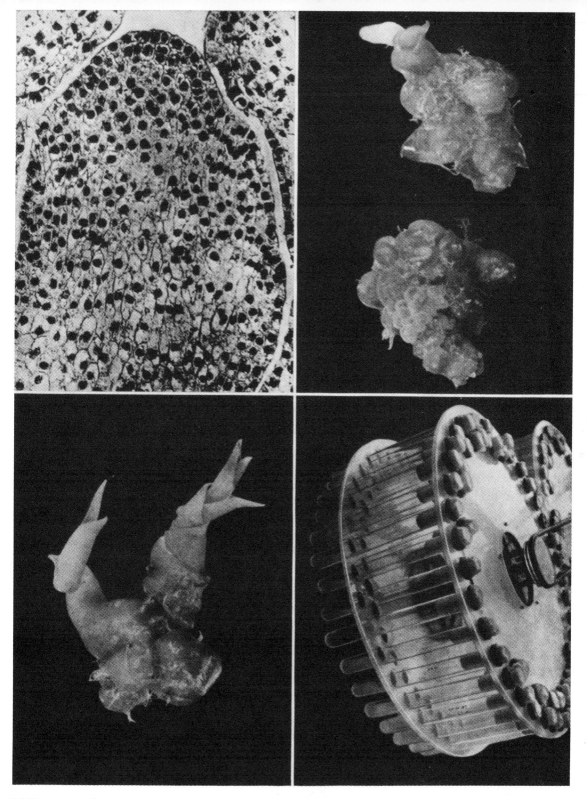

1 Microscopical cross-section through apical meristem of an orchid; 2 Groups of protocorms of Cymbidium; 3 Protocorm of Cymbidium with first leaves developing; 4 Test tubes in position on the klinostat

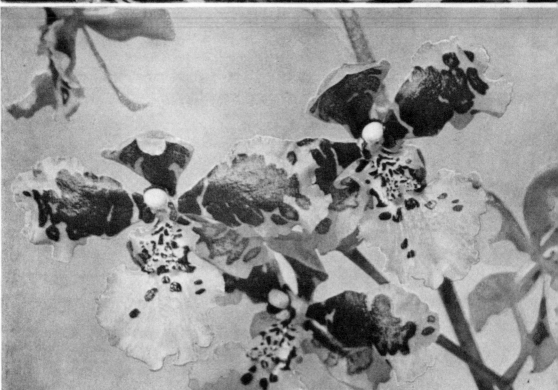

1 Odontoglossum grande; 2 Oncidium sarcodes

leaves and long pendulous spikes of mauve-pink or purple and white fragrant flowers.

A. crispa (India, Ceylon), III, plant up to 2 m (6½ ft.) high, flowers white, tinged rosy purple.

A. falcata (Burma, Thailand), III, terete leaves.

A. japonica (Japan), II, requires cooler conditions; flowers greenish-white, marked purple-violet.

A. odorata (tropical Asia), II, plant up to 2 m (6½ ft.) high.

A. vandarum (India), II, requires cooler conditions; terete leaves.

Aganisia

Epiphytic; 3 species, tropical America. Warm house with no definite resting period and much shade; compost B. Pseudobulbous with leaves up to about 25 cm (10 in.) and arching spikes of large flowers.

A. cyanea (Brazil, Colombia), III, flowers mauve on outer surface, deep azure blue inside, yellow crest on lip.

Angraecum

Epiphytic; 200 species, tropical Africa, Madagascar and Mascarenes. Warm or intermediate house with no resting period; compost F. Extremely diverse vegetatively but flowers always green or white, starlike, very variable in size.

A. distichum (tropical Africa), II, very small, thick leaves in two overlapping rows, pure white, very small flowers borne singly but often in considerable quantity.

A. eburneum (Madagascar, Mascarenes), II, very large plant, up to 2 m (6½ ft.) high, with leathery leaves up to 1 m (3 ft.) long: inflorescences longer than leaves, bearing many large white, waxy flowers up to 5 cm (2 in.) diam.

A. sesquipedale (Madagascar), II, stems erect, up to 0.5 m (1½ ft.) long, bearing two rows of long leaves and inflorescences about 0.5 m (1½ ft.) long with 2–4 creamy-white waxy flowers with spurs 35 cm (4 in.) long.

Anguloa

Epiphytic; 10 species, tropical America. Intermediate house with long water-free resting period in winter; compost A + 2 parts fibrous loam. Robust, pseudobulbous, with long leaves and single, short stemmed, large tulip-like waxy flowers.

A. clowesii (Colombia, Venezuela), II, flowers rich golden yellow.

A. uniflora (Colombia, Peru), II, flowers creamy-white flushed and spotted pink inside.

157

Anoectochilus

Terrestrial; 25 species, tropical Asia, Australia and Pacific Islands. Warm house with ample shade and high humidity, never allow to become too dry or too wet; compost C. Grown for their 'Jewel Orchid' leaves, ovate, deep velvety green with golden tessellation of 'veins', flowers dull white.

A. roxburghii (India, China), III.

A. regalis (Ceylon), I.

Ansellia

Epiphytic; 2 species, tropical Africa. Warm house with a month's resting period to ripen pseudobulbs; compost A + 1 part fibrous loam. Pseudobulbous, with tough long leaves, upwards pointing roots and long spikes of yellow and brown flowers about 3 cm (1¼ in.) across.

A. gigantea, II, flowers yellow with brownish-orange spots, often appearing more than once a year.

Arachnis

Epiphytic; 7 species, tropical Asia. Warm house with no resting period; compost F. Monopodial with short or very long stems, tough leathery leaves and long spikes of spider-like yellow and/or red flowers.

A. flos-aëris (Malesia), III, stems to 0.5 m (1½ ft.) long, leaves up to 20 cm (8 in.), flower spikes often branching, bearing numerous widely-spaced flowers about 8 cm (3⅛ in.) diameter, pale yellow-green with dark purple-brown blotchy markings.

A. maingayi (Malesia), III, similar to *A. flos-aëris* but flowers paler, almost white, with light purple or pinkish markings.

Armodorum

Epiphytic; 3 species, tropical Asia. Warm house with no resting period; compost F. Monopodial with long stems, leaves about 20 cm (8 in.) long and spikes of about 6 waxy flowers 4 cm (1½ in.) diameter.

A. labrosum (India, Burma), III, flowers yellow, blotched brownish-red.

Ascocentrum

Epiphytic; 6 species, tropical Asia. Warm house with no resting period; compost F. Monopodial with very short stems, short, closely packed stiff leaves and clusters of brightly coloured flowers.

158

A. ampullaceum (India, Burma, Thailand), III, deep rose-pink flowers.

A. curvifolium (India, Burma, Thailand), III, vermilion flowers.

A. miniatum (India, Java), III, orange flowers.

Ascoglossum

Epiphytic; 2 species, New Guinea, Solomon Islands. Warm house with no resting period; compost F. Monopodial with long stems, long leaves and large many-branched inflorescences bearing many flowers about 3 cm (1⅕ in.) diameter.

A. calopterum (New Guinea), III, flowers rich magenta-crimson.

Aspasia

Epiphytic; 10 species, tropical America. Intermediate house with short resting period after flowering; compost B. Pseudobulbous, with many leaves and erect inflorescences bearing several flowers about 5 cm (2 in.) diameter.

A. epidendroides (tropical America), II, sepals green with brown markings, petals pale lavender to greenish brown, lip white, veined lilac, crest yellow.

Barkeria

Epiphytic; 4 species, tropical America. Warm house with a long well marked resting period after flowering; compost B. Pseudobulbous with lanceolate to ovate leaves and arching inflorescences bearing up to 30 flowers up to 6 cm (2⅕ in.) diameter.

B. chinensis (Central America), II, flowers small, cream to pinkish.

B. elegans (Mexico), II, flowers large, tepals mallow-pink, lip white with purple blotch.

Batemannia

Epiphytic; 5 species, tropical America. Warm or intermediate house with little water in winter; compost B. Pseudobulbous with short leaves and short pendulous inflorescences bearing few waxy, fragrant flowers about 8 cm (3⅛ in.) diameter.

B. colleyi, II, flowers deep maroon to dull purplish-brown, lip white, flushed red.

Bifrenaria

Epiphytic; 10 species, tropical America. Cool or intermediate house with long resting period and plenty of sun to ripen new pseudobulbs; compost A. Pseudobulbous with single tough leaf up to 30 cm (12 in.) long and short inflorescence bearing very few, large strikingly coloured flowers.

159

B. harrisoniae, II, tepals creamy-white, lip rich wine-purple to dull magenta-maroon with bright yellow callus.

Bletilla

Terrestrial; 10 species, tropical Asia. Cool house or even alpine house with complete waterless rest during winter; compost E. Underground corms with long thin, glossy leaves and inflorescences about 30 cm (12 in.) long bearing several brightly coloured or white flowers.

B. striata (China, Japan), I (can be grown out-of-doors in sheltered, well-drained and sunny borders), flowers a brilliant rosy-magenta.

Bollea

Epiphytic; 3 species, tropical America. Cool house with adequate moisture at all times; compost B + $^1/_2$ part fibrous loam. Leaves arising bunched as a loose 'fan', each leaf up to 30 cm (12 in.) long, flowers borne singly on short pendulous stems, variously coloured.

B. coelestis (Colombia), III, flowers 10 cm (4 in.) diameter, deep violet blue with bright yellow callus on lip.

Brassavola

Epiphytic; 20 species, tropical America. Warm or intermediate house with no resting period; compost A, preferably in hanging baskets. Usually pseudobulbless plants and usually with long terete leaves and few-flowered inflorescences, flowers white, often delicately fringed.

B. cucullata, II, leaves up to 60 cm (24 in.) long, whip-like, flowers 10 cm (3 in.) diameter with long pendulous tails to sepals, petals and lip.

B. digbyana, III, pseudobulbous with solitary lanceolate leaf, 20 cm (8 in.) long, flowers 17 cm (6½ in.) diameter, pale yellowish-green, lip creamy-white heavily fringed, fragrant.

B. nodosa, II, thick, lanceolate leaves, white to greenish-white flowers, tepals slender, lip heart-shaped in upper half, flowering more than once a year.

Brassia

Epiphytic; 45 species, tropical America. Warm or intermediate house with no resting period; compost A. Pseudobulbous often with many long leaves and inflorescences bearing about a dozen spider-like flowers with very long, narrow tepals, usually yellowish-green and brown, and wide lip.

B. caudata, II, flowers up to 20 cm (8 in.) across, yellowish-green with dull brown spots, bars and other markings.

B. longissima, II, similar to *B. caudata* but flowers up to 50 cm (20 in.) across.

B. verrucosa, II, flowers pale green spotted deep greenish-black, lip with greenish-black warts.

Broughtonia

Epiphytic; 1 species, West Indies. Warm or intermediate house, plenty of light especially during resting period after flowering; compost A, must be well drained, e.g. raft culture. Pseudobulbous with paired leaves and inflorescences up to 60 cm (24 in.) long bearing up to 15 flowers 5 cm (2 in.) across, crimson.

B. sanguinea, II, flowers borne at all seasons vivid crimson, lip with rosy-purple veins.

Bulbophyllum

Epiphytic; 900 species, tropical regions, all continents. Warm or intermediate house, most species not requiring a long or well-marked resting period; compost B. Pseudobulbous with 1 or 2 leaves per bulb, inflorescences rising from base of pseudobulb, single to many-flowered, flowers variously coloured, lip hinged.

B. barbigerum (tropical Africa), II, pseudobulbs small, single leafed, leaf about 8 cm (3⅛ in.) long, 3 cm (1¼ in.) wide, inflorescence with about 15 flowers, flowers evil-smelling, dull purple, lip covered with very long stiff hairs so that it waves in the slightest breeze.

B. beccarii (Borneo), III, leaf up to 60 cm (24 in.) long, 20 cm (8 in.) wide flowers about 8 cm (3⅛ in.) across, foul smelling, fleshy, borne in great profusion yellowish-red.

B. lobbii (Burma, Malaya), II, plant slightly longer than B. *B. barbigerum* flowers borne singly, up to 10 cm (4 in.) across pale buff-yellow, spotted and lined red.

Calanthe

Terrestrial or epiphytic; 120 species, tropical Africa, tropical Asia to Australia and Pacific Islands. Cool, intermediate or warm house, with or without very dry resting period after flowering, depending on species; compost E for terrestrials, D for epiphytes. Pseudobulbs usually present, deciduous or evergreen, large leaves, dense spikes of small flowers ranging from purest white to deep golden-orange and dull pinkish-mauve.

161

C. masuca (tropical Asia), II, intermediate house with resting period, deciduous, pseudobulbous, leaves up to 30 cm (12 in.) long, flower spike 60 cm (24 in.), flowers pure-white to dark violet.

C. triplicata (India to Australia and Pacific Islands), III, warm house with no resting period, evergreen, pseudobulbless, grey-green leaves up to 60 cm (24 in.) long, flower spikes 60 cm (24 in.) tall, flowers small, pure white.

C. vestita (Malesia), II, cool or intermediate house with marked resting period after flowering, leaves to 45 cm (18 in.) long, flower spikes taller bearing up to 12 white flowers with rosy-pink labellums.

Catasetum

Terrestrial or epiphytic; 70 species, tropical America. Warm or intermediate house with decided rest in winter; compost A + 2 parts loam. Pseudobulbous, bearing up to 6 leaves at top, flower spikes erect or pendulous, flowers greenish or yellow, often tinged dull red, male, female or hermaphrodite, pollinia violently ejected when sensitive horns of column touched.

C. fimbriatum, III, very odd looking flowers, pale greenish-yellow, heavily marked dull reddish-purple transverse spots.

C. macrocarpum, III, sepals and petals folded together to produce tulip-like structure, green with purple spots, lip yellow.

C. pileatum, III, flowers opening flat, up to 10 cm (4 in.) across, heavily scented, creamy-white to pale yellow.

Cattleya

Epiphytic; 60 species, tropical America. Intermediate or warm house, slight rest with less water when dormant; compost A. Pseudobulbous, with 1 or 2 or more leaves, inflorescences single or few-flowered, flowers very large and showy, usually lilac mauve with some deeper purple and yellow. (N.B. all species are well worth cultivating):

C. bowringiana (British Honduras), II, pseudobulbs very thin, to 1 m (3 ft.) tall, 2–4 leaves, inflorescence many-flowered, flowers 8 cm ($3\frac{1}{8}$ in.) across, rose magenta.

C. citrina (Mexico), III, rounded pseudobulbs bearing 2 dull grey-green pendulous leaves and single-flowered inflorescences, flowers pure yellow.

C. dowiana (Costa Rica), II, very large flowers, sepals and petals clear yellow, suffused magenta, lip crimson magenta, gold veined.

C. dowiana var-aurea (Brazil), II, similar to *C. dowiana* but sepals and petals not flecked or suffused magenta.

162

C. guttata (Brazil), III, sepals and petals yellow-green, spotted red, lip white or rosy-purple.

C. intermedia (Brazil), II, sepals and petals lavender to pale rose, lip white with magenta and yellow markings.

C. labiata (Brazil), II, flowers up to 15 cm (6 in.) across, sepals and petals bright lilac-pink, lip crimson magenta.

C. mossiae (Venezuela), II, larger and brighter-coloured version of *C. labiata*.

C. trianaei (Colombia), II, superior version of *C. labiata*.

Cattleyopsis

Epiphytic; 2 species, West Indies. Warm house with short rest after flowering; compost A. Pseudobulbous, dwarf plants, with small Cattleya-like flowers.

C. lindenii, III, pseudobulbs small, leaves up 12 cm (5 in.) long, inflorescences to 1 m (3 ft.) bearing up to 12 flowers, sepals and petals pale rose-pink, lip deep rose veined crimson, yellow throat.

Chysis

Epiphytic; 6 species, tropical America. Intermediate house with slightly less water during resting period; compost C, preferably in hanging basket. Pseudobulbous, many-leaved, flowers large, yellowish.

C. aurea (Central America), III, pseudobulbs 30 cm (12 in.) tall, flowers up to 12 cm (5 in.) across, tawny-yellow, lip heavily marked scarlet.

C. bractescens (Central America), III, similar to *C. aurea* but larger, sepals and petals creamy-white, lip yellow, lightly marked.

Cirrhopetalum

Epiphytic; 70 species, tropical Africa, Asia, Australia and Pacific Islands. Warm or intermediate house with slight rest after flowering; compost B. Pseudobulbous, closely resembling Bulbophyllum but flowers massed in umbels, lateral sepals often elongated, joined, all colours except blue.

C. gracillimum (Malesia, Pacific Islands), II, flowers deep crimson, lateral sepals very long and thin.

C. medusae (Malesia), II, umbels, a mop-like head of 50 or more cream, spotted pink, flowers with very long lateral sepals.

C. umbellatum (East Africa to Australia and Pacific Islands), II, up to 10 flowers per head, strap-shaped lateral sepals, from pure yellow spotted red to crimson.

163

Cochleanthes

Epiphytic; 14 species, tropical America. Intermediate house with no resting period; compost B + 2 parts loam. Leaves arrayed fan-like, flowers produced singly at base of plant, usually coloured white, and shades of purple and violet.

C. discolor (Central America), II, sepals white, petals white suffused pale violet, lip deep violet, callus large, white.

Cochlioda

Epiphytic; 6 species, tropical America. Cool house with no marked resting period; compost B. Pseudobulbous, with leaves up to 30 cm (12 in.) long, long arching many-flowered inflorescences. Of little use as horticultural subjects as such but the brilliant reds, crimsons and scarlets of the flowers have meant that they have been frequently hybridized with species of other genera.

Coelogyne

Epiphytic; 200 species, tropical Asia and Pacific Islands. Cool, intermediate or warm house with differing degrees and lengths of resting period depending on origin of species; compost A. Pseudobulbous, with lanceolate, stiff leaves and erect or pendulous flower spikes, flowers white, yellow, orange, green or salmon, often marked red and chestnut.

C. asperata (Malesia), III, leaves up to 60 cm (24 in.) long, up to 15 flowers borne on pendulous stem bearing showy bracts, sepals and petals pale buff-green to creamy-white, lip white or cream, heavily marked deep rust-red and yellow.

C.cristata (Himalayas), I, ideal for window-sill culture, flowers pure white shaded deep yellow-orange towards centre of lip.

C. virescens (Indo-China, Thailand), II, flowers rich apple green, lip heavily marked black.

Comparettia

Epiphytic; 7 species, tropical America. Warm house with no resting period; compost B. Pseudobulbous (pseudobulbs very small), large leaved, inflorescences erect or arching, few-flowered, flowers scarlet or crimson.

C. falcata, II, flowers 3 cm (1½ in.) across, vivid magenta-rose.

Cycnoches

Epiphytic; 12 species, tropical America. Warm or intermediate house with decided rest in winter; compost A + 2 parts loam. Pseudobulbous, large-leaved (deciduous),

164

1 Ophrys fuciflora; 2 Cypripedium speciosum; 3 Angulocaste Olympus;
4 Miltonia Celle 'Feuerwerk'; 5 Vuylstekeara hybrid; 6 Trigonidium seemannii

1 Cirrhopetalum; 2 Epidendrum ciliare;
3 Dendrochilum cobbianum; 4 Dendrobium aphyllum (D. pierardii)

1 Pleione maculata; **2** Trichopilia tortilis; **3** Macodes petola

1 Cephalanthera rubra; **2** Aceras anthropophora; **3** Cypripedium acaule;
4 Orchis mascula; **5** Gymnadenia conopsea; **6** Epipactis palustris;
7 Orchis simia; **8** Anacamptis pyramidalis; **9** Ophrys apifera

inflorescences few- or many-flowered, flowers large or small, male, female or herm-aphrodite.

C. chlorochilon, III, flowers very large, up to 13 cm (5 in.) across, sepals and petals rich green, lip large, white, column of male flowers very long and 'swan' like.

C. egertonianum, III, male flowers green, spotted maroon or brown, produced on pendulous spikes up to 60 cm (2 ft.) long, female flowers very rarely produced, large, yellow-green.

Cymbidium

Terrestrial or epiphytic; 40 species, tropical Asia and Australia. Cool or inter-mediate house, plenty of shade, with watering considerably reduced during flower-ing; compost D. Pseudobulbous, leaves arising on both sides of pseudobulb, leaves up to 60 cm (24 in.) long, flower spikes erect, pendulous or arching, often very long, bearing from 1 to 80 flowers, large and small, variously coloured.

C. eburneum (India), II, large leaves, inflorescences erect, flowers up to 8 cm (3⅛ in.) across, pure white, centre of lip marked orange-yellow.

C. lowianum (Burma), large leaves, inflorescences up to 1·5 m (5 ft.) long, flowers large, sepals and petals yellow-green, streaked pale brown, lip creamy-white, margin deep rich red.

C. tracyanum (Burma), II, medium-sized leaves, flowers up to 15 cm (6 in.) across, greenish- or brownish-yellow, spotted brown, lip yellow spotted brown.

Cyrtopodium

Terrestrial; 10 species, tropical America. Intermediate or warm house with rest after flowering; compost E. Pseudobulbs very large, bearing several large deciduous leaves towards apex, inflorescences erect, very long, bearing many yellow, red and brown flowers.

C. punctatum, III, inflorescence up to 125 cm (3 ft.) tall, heavily branched, bearing up to 200 flowers up to 5 cm (2 in.) across, sepals and petals pale yellowish-green spotted red, lip deep reddish-brown, crest yellow.

Dendrobium

Epiphytic; 1200 species, tropical Asia, Australia and Pacific Islands. Warm, inter-mediate or cool house, deciduous species requiring a long dry rest after flowering, evergreen species not to be allowed to dry out; compost A. Pseudobulbs ranging from almost spherical to reedlike, leaves borne in two rows along stem or elon-

169

gated pseudobulb, inflorescences variable, from 1 to over 100 flowered, flowers in all colours including blue.

D. aggregatum (tropical Asia), II, intermediate house, deciduous dwarf plants with pendulous spikes up of to 12 flowers, each about 5 cm (2 in.) across, deep orange-yellow.

D. bigibbum (Australia), II, warm house, evergreen large plants, up to 1·6 m (5⅓ ft.) tall, with inflorescences up to 1·8 m (6 ft.) tall bearing large, dark-rose shaded magenta flowers.

D. nobile (tropical Asian mainland), II, cool house, evergreen, medium sized plants bearing flowers singly, in pairs or threes all along stem, flowers white, tipped rosy-magenta, lip white, throat deepest magenta.

Dendrochilum

Epiphytic; 100 species, tropical Asia. Warm or intermediate house, with differing degrees and lengths of resting periods depending on origin of species; compost A. Pseudobulbous with 1 leaf per pseudobulb, flowers yellow or creamy-white neatly arrayed in two rows on very slender, drooping spikes at top of erect stem.

D. filiforme (Philippines), II, flower spike up to 60 cm (24 in.) long, many-flowered, flowers yellowish-white, lip yellow, very fragrant.

D. glumaceum (Philippines), II, flower spike up to 40 cm (16 in.) long, many-flowered, bearing conspicuous bracts, flowers up to 2.5 cm (1 in.) across, creamy-white, lip yellowish-green.

Diacrium

Epiphytic; 2 species, tropical America. Warm or intermediate house, with no resting but always kept fairly dry; compost A. Pseudobulbous with erect spikes of large creamy-white flowers.

D. bicornutum, III, pseudobulbs up to 30 cm (12 in.) tall, flowers up to 8 cm (3⅛ in.) across, lip faintly spotted purple.

Disa

Terrestrial; 130 species, tropical Africa, Madagascar and the Mascarenes. Erect shoots arise from rootstock bearing long leaves and flower spikes, flowers blue, red, yellow or orange. Only 1 species can be grown.

D. uniflora (South Africa), III, cool house, brief resting period; compost E. Up to 5 flowers, 10 cm (4 in.) across, scarlet or orange-red, very showy.

Doritis

Epiphytic; 1 species, tropical Asia. Warm house with no resting period; compost F. Monopodial with long narrow leaves and upright flower spike.

D. pulcherrima, II, up to 15 flowers, up to 3 cm (1⅓ in.) across, ranging from pale pinkish-mauve to deep rich magenta.

Epidendrum

Terrestrial or epiphytic; 400 species, tropical America. Warm, intermediate or cool house, with or without marked resting period, depending on origin of species; compost A. Pseudobulbous or reed-like, several- to many-flowered inflorescences, flowers large or small, in all colours.

E. atropurpureum, II, warm house, without resting period, ovoid pseudobulbs up to 10 cm (4 in.) tall, leaves thick, strap-shaped, up to 45 cm (18 in.) long, inflorescence bearing 4–20 flowers, sepals and petals chocolate-brown, lip white, veined magenta.

E. cochleatum, II, intermediate house without resting period, sepals and petals long, narrow, twisted, pale yellowish-green, lip dark velvety purple, shell-shaped.

E. ibaguense (tropical America, naturalized in many tropical regions), II, intermediate house without resting period, reed-like with short leaves and dense terminal inflorescences, flowers orange-red, yellow, crimson or white.

E. mariae (Mexico), III, similar generally to *E. atropurpureum* but flowers much longer, sepals and petals rich yellowish-green, lip pure white.

Eria

Epiphytic; 375 species, tropical Asia, Australia and Pacific Islands. Warm or intermediate house without marked resting period; compost A or B. Pseudobulbous (usually) varying greatly in size, flowers usually in dense inflorescences, pure white through pinks, yellows and greens to dull ginger-brown, often mealy or hairy.

E. amica, II, intermediate house, flowers creamy-white to pale greenish-yellow, sepals and petals veined red, lip bearing two bright yellow lobes.

E. coronaria (Himalayas), II, intermediate house, sepals and petals pure white, lip side-lobes purple veined, middle-lobe yellow.

E. floribunda (Malesia), III, warm house, non-pseudobulbous, stem to 40 cm (16 in.) tall, flower spikes 20 cm (8 in.) long, bearing 50 or more white, delicately flushed pink, flowers.

171

Eulophia

Terrestrial; 200 species, all tropical regions. Warm or intermediate house, very marked resting period especially with the hard-pseudobulbed species; compost E. Pseudobulbous (usually), with long, narrow leaves (if any), flower spikes generally very tall, many-flowered, flowers white, yellow, orange, red, mauve, purple or brown, varying greatly in size.

E. alta (tropical Africa, tropical America), III, non-pseudobulbous, leaves and flower spikes up to 1 · 3 m (4 ft.) tall, flowers greenish and purple.

E. quartiniana (tropical Africa), II, rich green leaves, up to 45 cm (18 in.) tall, flowers greenish and rich pink-magenta.

Eulophiella

Terrestrial; 4 species, Madagascar. Warm house with no resting period; compost C. Pseudobulbous, leaves up to 60 cm (24 in.) long, inflorescences several-flowered, flowers large.

E. elisabethae, III, sepals and petals white, flushed rose, lip white and yellow.

Gongora

Epiphytic; 20 species, tropical America. Warm or intermediate house with no well-defined resting period; compost B. Pseudobulbous, with long leaves, pendulous inflorescences up to 80 cm (32 in.) long, bearing many very bizarrely shaped flowers.

G. quinquenervis, II, flowers very bizarre, pure yellow or pinkish-brick, often spotted red.

Grammangis

Epiphytic; 1 species, Madagascar. Warm house with no resting period; compost D. Pseudobulbous, with inflorescences up to 1 m (3 ft.) long, many-flowered.

G. ellisii, III, flowers up to 8 cm (3⅛ in.) across, sepals shining chestnut-brown, petals and lip white with rose-red markings.

Grammatophyllum

Terrestrial or epiphytic; 10 species, tropical Asia. Warm house with no resting period; compost F. Pseudobulbous, sometimes up to 9 m (30 ft.) long, leaves often up to 1 · 7 m (70 in.) long, inflorescences up to 2.5 m (8 ft.) long bearing up to 100 or more flowers, flowers usually dull yellows and browns.

G. scriptum (Malesia), III, relatively small species, flowers 7 cm (3 in.) across, yellow-green, heavily spotted red-brown.

G. speciosum (Malesia), III, largest species of orchid in the world, flowers up to 20 cm (8 in.) across, golden-yellow, blotched and spotted reddish-brown.

Habenaria

Terrestrial (usually); 600 species, all tropical regions. Warm, intermediate or cool house, with or without resting period, depending on origin of species; compost E. Tuberous, with leafy aerial stems bearing few to many flowers, white, green or rarely shades of red.

H. procera (tropical Africa), III, warm house, usually epiphytic, up to 60 cm (24 in.) tall, bearing many long-spurred white flowers.

H. rhodocheila (tropical Asia), III, warm house, sepals and petals green, lip large, yellow, orange or vermilion.

Haemaria

Terrestrial; 1 species, tropical Asia. Warm house with no resting period; compost C. 'Jewel' orchid with deep velvety green leaf, veined coppery-gold, deep purple on under surface, inflorescence up to 30 cm (2 in.) tall, flowers white.

H. discolor, III, various forms with different coloured leaves are grown.

Helcia

Epiphytic; 1 species (Colombia, Ecuador). Cool house with short but marked resting period; compost D. Pseudobulbous, flowers borne singly, up to 9 cm (3½ in.) across, sepals and petals olive-green with transverse bands of dull maroon-brown, lip white, veined crimson.

H. sanguinolenta, III.

Huntleya

Epiphytic; 10 species, tropical America. Cool or intermediate house with no resting period; compost B. Leaves arranged fan-like, flowers very shiny, browns, yellows, and white, often spotted.

H. meleagris, III, flowers up to 13 cm (5⅛ in.) across, sepals and petals shiny reddish-brown, slightly spotted purple, lip white or yellowish, front half as petals.

Jumellea

Epiphytic; 45 species, tropical Africa and Madagascar. Warm house with no resting period; compost F. Monopodial, very varied vegetatively, flowers long spurred, white or cream.

J. sagittata (Madagascar), III, long strap-shaped leaves and pure white flowers.

173

Laelia

Epiphytic; 30 species, tropical America. Cool, intermediate or warm house, with or without resting period after flowering; compost A. Pseudobulbous (usually) from very small to 25 cm (10 in.) tall, leaves thick, leathery, strap-shaped or terete, flower spikes bearing one to many flowers, usually large and colourful.

L. anceps (Mexico), II, intermediate house with long, cool rest after flowering. Flowers up to 10 cm (4 in.) across, pale rosy-purple, lip striped and veined yellow and purple, many cultivars are grown.

L. cinnabarina (Brazil), III, flowers up to 8 cm (3⅛ in.) across, bright orange-red.

L. purpurata (Brazil), III, flowers up to 22 cm (8½ in.) across, sepals and petals white, lip dark velvety maroon-purple with yellow patch, many cultivars are grown.

L. xanthina (Brazil), III, flowers bright-yellow, lip streaked purple.

Laeliopsis

Epiphytic; 2 species, West Indies. Warm house with short resting period; compost A. Pseudobulbous, with branched inflorescence with up to 10 large flowers.

L. domingensis, III, inflorescence up to 60 cm (24 in.) long, flowers 7 cm (2¾ in.) across, sepals and petals pale rosy mauve with purple veins, lip white and yellow, purple lined transversely.

Lycaste

Epiphytic (usually); 45 species, tropical America. Cool or intermediate house with well-marked resting period; compost E. Pseudobulbous, single flowers arise in great profusion on short stems from base of pseudobulbs, flowers large, green, yellow, orange, red or white, very heavily scented.

L. aromatica (Central America), II, flowers waxy, up to 8 cm (3⅛ in.) across, golden orange-yellow.

L. barringtoniae (West Indies), II, sepals and petals olive-green, fringed lip pale brownish buff.

L. deppei (Central America), II, flowers large, sepals pale green lightly mottled and flushed red, petals white, lip middle-lobe chrome yellow, side lobes white, all three lobes spotted red.

L. virginalis (Central America), III, flowers up to 15 cm (6 in.) across, white, variously veined, flushed and spotted violet-pink.

Masdevallia

Epiphytic; 275 species, tropical America. Cool or intermediate house with no well marked resting period; compost B. Tufted, sepals relatively large, nearly always joined together to form a tube in which the very small petals and lip are more or less concealed, long tails usually on sepals, flower colours ranging from pure white to deepest maroon-black.

M. bella, II, sepals tawny yellow, heavily spotted brown, lip white, shell-like.

M. coccinea, II, flowers varying from orange and scarlet to deep magenta, crimson and purple.

Maxillaria

Terrestrial or epiphytic; 300 species, tropical America. Cool or intermediate house with no well-marked resting period; compost B. Pseudobulbous, tufted or creeping, flowers borne singly, large or very small, from pure-white to deep blood-red.

M. camardii, II, intermediate house, creeping or pendulous, flowers pure white except for yellow inside lip.

M. nasuta, II, intermediate house, star-like flowers, petals and sepals pale yellow green, suffused maroon on back; lip deep maroon, yellow tip.

M. picta, II, cool house, flowers yellow, strangely randomly spotted and flecked purple and pale red.

Miltonia

Epiphytic; 25 species, tropical America. Cool or intermediate house with no marked resting period; compost B. Pseudobulbous, leaves yellow-green or blue-green, almost silvery, flowers usually flattened (pansy-like), ranging from pure-white through pink to deep brick-red and from yellow to browns and purples.

M. candida, III, intermediate house, sepals greenish-yellow, petals bright yellow, marked reddish-brown, lip white with purple blotches.

M. regnellii, III, cool house, sepals and petals white, lip pale rose, streaked rosy purple, crest pale yellow, var. **citrina** has yellow sepals and petals.

M. spectabilis, III, intermediate house, sepals and petals creamy white, tinged pink, lip bright rose-purple veined deep purple.

M. vexillaria, III., cool house, sepals and petals pale rosy-mauve, lip similar but veined bright yellow.

175

Mormodes

Epiphytic; 30 species, tropical America. Intermediate or warm house with well-defined resting period; compost A + 2 parts fibrous loam. Pseudobulbous, resembling Catasetum, but with hermaphrodite flowers only, flowers twisted, especially column, yellow white or brownish-red to purplish-green, often spotted.

M. buccinator, III, pseudobulbs up to 15 cm (6 in.) tall, flower spike slightly taller, flowers very variable in colour, from pale green and white to dull buff, heavily spotted red-brown.

M. colossus, III, pseudobulbs up to 30 cm (12 in.) tall, flower spike twice as long, flowers up to 8 cm (3⅛ in.) across, sepals and petals shades of greenish-brown or cream, lip brownish-yellow.

Odontoglossum

Epiphytic (usually); 200 species, tropical America. Cool, intermediate or warm house, depending on origin of species no marked resting period; compost B. Pseudobulbous, often large-leaved, flower spikes short or long bearing few to many flowers, usually white, yellow-brown or mauve.

O. crispum (Colombia), II, large plants, sepals and petals white, faintly suffused pale rose, unevenly spotted reddish-brown, lip white, yellow and red marks.

O. grande (Central America), II, flowers very large, sepals and petals reddish-brown, lip creamy, flecked brown.

Oncidium

Epiphytic; 300 species, tropical America. Cool, intermediate or warm house, depending on origin of species with a short resting period for various species; compost A. Pseudobulbous, leaves often long, inflorescences up to 4 m (13 ft.) long, often scrambling, flowers small, usually yellow, marked pale chestnut brown.

O. ornithorrhynchum, II, intermediate house, flowers small, dull lilac-mauve.

O. papilio, III, intermediate house, flower spike up to 1–3 m (3–9 ft.) high, flowers opening singly in succession, dorsal sepal and petals erect, long and narrow, dull red, lateral and lip red-brown with yellow markings.

O. varicosum, III, intermediate house, sepals and petals small, lip very large and bright yellow.

Paphiopedilum

Terrestrial; 50 species, tropical Asia, Pacific Islands. Cool, intermediate or warm house with no marked resting period; compost B and C. Leaves arrayed in a loose

176

'fan', either uniformly green or blue-green, pale green tessellated, flowers born singly or up to 6 on a spike, lateral sepals joined to form a synsepalum, lip pouch-shaped, flower colours yellow, green or brown to violet, purple or maroon, or creamy-white, usually 'candy striped'.

P. barbatum, II, intermediate house, tessellated leaves, 1 or 2 flowers per spike, dorsal sepal greenish-white streaked purple, petals greenish with hairy crimson warts, lip deep purplish brown.

P. callosum, II, intermediate or warm house, similar to *P. barbatum* but dorsal sepal pure white streaked purple.

P. fairieanum, III, intermediate house, uniformly green leaves, flowers basically maroon and white striped and veined, very crinkled edge to petals.

P. insigne, I, cool house, uniformly green leaves, dorsal sepal apex white, remainder apple-green with numerous dull purplish-brown spots, petals greenish-yellow striped purplish-brown, lip yellowish-green, flushed pale brown.

P. rothschildianum, III, warm house, uniformly green leaves, leaves and inflorescence up to 60 cm (24 in.) long, up to 5 flowers, sepals pale yellowish-white longitudinally striped purplish-brown, lip brownish-yellow, column staminode resembling spider's leg, 6 cm (2⅓ in.) long.

Phaius

Terrestrial or epiphytic; 50 species, tropical Africa, Asia, Australia and Pacific Islands. Warm or intermediate house with short resting period only; compost E. Pseudobulbous or rhizomatous, leaves usually very long, 1 to several flowers on long inflorescence, flowers white, yellow, orange and brown to dull purplish-mauve.

P. tancarvilliae (Tropical Asia), II, leaves up to 1.3 m (3⅓ ft.) high, flower spike up to 1.6 m (5⅓ ft.), up to 20 flowers 10 cm (4 in.) across, sepals and petals white on outside, red-brown inside, lip dark wine red.

Phalaenopsis

Epiphytic; 35 species, tropical Asia and Australia. Warm house with no resting period; compost F. Monopodial, short-stemmed, flowers large or small born singly or up to 80 on a spike, often 'moth'-like, purest white to dull reddish-brown and mauve.

P. amabilis (tropical Asia, Australia), III, flowers large, pure white with red and yellow markings on complex lip.

P. lueddemanniana (Philippines), III, flowers small, sepals brown shaded mauve, petals amethyst, lip yellow, white and magenta.

177

Pleione

Terrestrial; 9 species, tropical Asia. Cool house with well marked resting period after leaves die, most species can also be grown in alpine house, cold-frames or window sills; compost E. Pseudobulbous, deciduous, flowers borne singly or in pairs, somewhat resembling miniature Cattleyas, white, yellow, or shades of mauve and lilac pink.

P. formosana (Formosa), I, can be grown in sheltered portions in rock gardens in warmer parts of country, flowers pure white or sepals and petals mauve-pink, lip paler, spotted brick-red, ginger or yellow, fringed.

P. humilis (India, Burma), I, similar to *P. formosana* but flowers very pale blush pink, lip heavily spotted crimson, amethyst or vermilion.

P. praecox (India, Burma), I, barrel-shaped pseudobulbs, spotted green and purple, flowers deep rosy pink.

Pleurothallis

Epiphytic; 1000 species, tropical America. Cool or intermediate house with no resting period; compost B. Tufted, leaves large to very small, flowers variously borne, from long inflorescences to single flowers with stalk immersed in leaf blade.
P. ghiesbreghtiana, II, plants up to 60 cm (24 in.) tall, long inflorescences bearing many fragrant, translucent yellow-green flowers.

Polystachya

Epiphytic; 200 species, tropical regions, mainly Africa. Cool, intermediate or warm house, some species requiring a resting period, rarely seen in cultivation: compost B. Pseudobulbous, tufted or scrambling or reed-like, flowers usually small and dull coloured.

P. bella (tropical Africa), III, warm house with slight resting period in winter, long erect spike of bright yellow, downwards pointing flowers.

Renanthera

Epiphytic; 15 species, tropical Asia and Pacific Islands. Warm house with no resting period; compost F. Monopodial, long stems, short oblong leaves, flower spike usually branched bearing many spider-like red or red and yellow flowers.

R. imschootiana, III, flowers 2 cm ($\frac{3}{4}$ in.) across, yellow, spotted red.

Rhynchostylis

Epiphytic; 15 species, tropical Asia. Warm or intermediate house with no resting period; compost F. Monopodial with short stems, long leaves and long pendulous inflorescences densely many-flowered.

R. retusa, III, sepals and petals white, spotted purple, lip purple.

178

Rodriguezia

Epiphytic; 30 species, tropical America. Warm or intermediate house with no resting period; compost B. Pseudobulbous, flower spikes with many small but brightly coloured flowers.

R. secunda, III, flowers deep rose pink.

Sarcochilus

Epiphytic; 40 species, tropical Asia, Australia and Pacific Islands. Warm, intermediate or cool house with no resting period; compost F. Monopodial, short stems, flowers small, often on dense spikes, basically cream or white with various red, yellow or brown spots and markings.

S. falcatus (Australia), II, cool house, preferably on blocks, flowers up to 2 cm ($\frac{3}{4}$ in.) across, creamy-white, lip side-lobes flushed orange, veined deep-red, middle lobe flushed yellow, purple flecked.

Sobralia

Terrestrial; 90 species, tropical America. Warm or intermediate house with brief resting period; compost E. Reed-like, up to 3 m (10 ft.) high, relatively short leaves evenly spaced along stem, flowers rather flappy, large, lasting a short time only, brightly coloured.

S. macrantha, III, flowers up to 20 cm (8 in.) across, deep rosy-purple, lip marked yellow inside.

Sophronitis

Epiphytic; 6 species, Brazil. Intermediate house with no marked resting period; compost C. Pseudobulbous, pseudobulbs very small, flowers borne singly, pink to deep scarlet.

S. coccinea, III, flowers up to 7 cm ($2\frac{3}{4}$ in.) across, brilliant scarlet.

Spathoglottis

Terrestrial; 50 species, tropical Asia and Pacific Islands. Cool, intermediate or warm house with well defined resting period for deciduous species; compost E. Pseudobulbous, with erect leaves and spikes bearing one to many flowers ranging from pure white to deepest mauve-purple.

S. plicata, II, leaves and flower spikes to 1 m (3 ft.) high, up to 50 flowers per spike, some in bud, some in flower, some in capsule and some as dehisced capsules, pale mauve-pink, lip deep magenta, crests yellow.

179

Stanhopea

Epiphytic; 45 species, tropical America. Warm or intermediate house with only slight resting period; compost A. Pseudobulbous, highly complex flowers appearing at base of pseudobulbs (plants should be grown in hanging baskets, the flowers protruding through base), creamy white to buff orange, spotted or blotched deep maroon.

S. graveolens, II, flowers up to 12 cm (5 in.) across, pale yellow heavily marked deep maroon.

S. wardii, II, similar to *S. graveolens* but flowers only lightly spotted.

Stelis

Epiphytic; 250 species, tropical America. Cool or intermediate house with no resting period. Tufted, leaves small, flowers in erect spikes, very small, flat, self-coloured, petals, lip and column much smaller than sepals. True 'botanicals', dull, but very easily grown and flowered.

S. argentata, II.

S. hymenantha, II.

S. ophioglossoides, II.

Trichopilia

Epiphytic; 30 species, tropical America. Warm or intermediate house with no resting period; compost A. Pseudobulbous, with up to 5 flowers borne near base of pseudobulb, sepals and petals long, narrow, always twisted, lip large, frilled.

T. suavis, III, flowers up to 10 cm (4 in.) across, creamy-white, spotted pink.

Vanda

Epiphytic; 60 species, tropical Asia. Warm or intermediate house with only very brief resting period; compost F. Monopodial, short or long stemmed, leaves strap-shaped or terete, short or long, flowers variable in size and colour.

V. coerulea (N. India, Burma), III, stem up to 3.5 m (10 ft.), leaves up to 15 flowers per spike, 10 cm (4 in.) across, sepals and petals pastel-blue obscurely tessellated, lip deep purple-blue.

V. teres (N. India, Burma), III, stem up to 3.5 m (11⅓ ft.), leaves up to 13 cm (5 in.) long, terete, sepals white tinged purple; petals rosy-magenta, lip side-lobes yellowish-orange marked red, mid-lobe deep reddish purple.

V. tricolor (Java), III, stem up to 2 m (6⅔ ft.), leaves up to 50 cm (20 in.) long, flowers white or cream to pale mauve, heavily spotted reddish-brown, lip side-lobes white, mid-lobe white, reddish-brown and magenta-purple.

Vandopsis

Epiphytic; 20 species, tropical Asia and Pacific Islands. Warm or intermediate house with no resting period; compost F. Monopodial, short or long stemmed, Vanda-like flowers.

V. gigantea (Burma to Malaya), III, stem up to 30 cm (12 in.), leaves up to 60 cm (24 in.), very thick, spikes bearing up to 18 flowers, 8 cm (3⅛ in.) across, yellow with brown markings.

V. lissochiloides (Philippines), III, stem up to 2 cm (¾ in.), leaves up to 60 cm (24 in.), very thick, spikes bearing up to 30 flowers, 8 cm (3⅛ in.) across, yellow heavily spotted and blotched magenta purple.

Vanilla

Epiphytic; 100 species, tropical regions. Warm or intermediate house with no resting period; compost F. Leafy or leafless scramblers or climbers, large 'lily-like' flowers up to 15 cm (6 in.) across, white, yellow or green, marked reddish-purple.

V. imperialis (tropical Africa), III, leaves up to 25 cm (10 in.) long, 12 cm (5 in.) broad, flowers opening 1 or 2 at a time, large, yellow or cream, lip heavily blotched rosy purple.

V. planifolia (Central America, cultivated throughout the tropics), leaves up to 20 cm (8 in.) long, flowers greenish-white, seed pods 15 cm (6 in.) long used for commercial flavouring extract after fermentation.

Xylobium

Epiphytic; 30 species, tropical America. Cool or intermediate house with no well defined resting period; compost B. Pseudobulbous with long leaves and short dense spikes of small, generally dull flowers.

X. squalens, III, leaves up to 60 cm (24 in.) long, sepals and petals cream, flushed red, lip dark maroon.

Zygopetalum

Terrestrial or epiphytic; 25 species, tropical America. Cool or intermediate house with short but well defined resting period; compost F. Pseudobulbous with long leaves, and tall many-flowered spike of fragrant flowers, purple, white and green.

Z. intermedium (Brazil), III, sepals and petals yellowish-green, blotched brown, lip white, longitudinally striped deep blue.

ORCHIDS IN THE GARDEN

Most of this book has dealt with the orchids of the tropical and subtropical regions of the world. This is to be expected as in north America and Europe no more than $3^1/_2$ per cent of the 17,000 species of orchids actually occur. Although we are no doubt, as tropical orchid enthusiasts, also familiar with our native species we have very little knowledge of their cultivation. This too is hardly surprising since there is usually little desire to cultivate them, their beauty and attraction being not so much as individual plants but when seen en masse in their natural settings or when revealed in stark beauty under the lens.

When seen in the wild it is usual to speculate on how well they would grow in the garden but it is difficult actually to do this. Orchids are an exception to the rule that wild plants do better in the care and protection of the garden than they do in the wild. It is relatively easy to simulate most environmental factors in a garden but soil conditions which are so essential to the well-being of terrestrial orchids and their mycorrhiza are much more difficult to re-create adequately.

Nevertheless many gardeners attempt to cultivate the native orchids of their home country or those of the surrounding countries in which they may have travelled on business or holiday. Occasionally the immediate results are good, the species seems at home and flowers profusely but, in nearly every case, it will suddenly die out without warning after only three or perhaps even after as many as ten or twelve years. Whether this is due to incorrect cultivation or because the plant has, anyway, come to the end of its life span is not known for sure, but what we do know is that the enthusiast then goes to collect, or perhaps buy, another plant in replacement. Not many years ago these replacements and, of course, the original plants were usually obtained by digging up orchids from the wild. However, this practice is now rightly condemned since the orchids that have survived this increasingly popular activity are succumbing to more widespread environmental changes such as drainage and pollution. Native European and north American temperate orchids should only be obtained by division of plants already in cultivation or from dealers of unimpeachable reputation who have raised their stocks in the same way. Many countries have legislation aimed at completely prohibiting the digging-up and removal of native orchids, but the practice still goes on. At the time of writing it is possible that there are no more Ladies' Slipper orchids, *Cypripedium calceolus*, remaining in Britain, the only two authenticated plants having been dug-up by an unscrupulous plant collector.

When cultivating temperate orchids of the northern hemisphere two main factors must be borne in mind. Firstly, not being under anything like the controlled conditions of either a greenhouse or even merely a window sill the climate of the area in which they are to be grown must be very carefully evaluated. Although many native north American species grow well in Britain and other parts of Europe, e.g. *Cypripedium reginae*, many species from that continent and from parts of Europe would not thrive at all in Britain. If one wishes to grow the species native to the Mediterranean region, and there are many well worth cultivating from there, it would be better to keep them either in cold frames or, better still, in an alpine house. In fact a very cool, rarely artificially heated, greenhouse, usually termed an alpine house is very good for cultivating all temperate orchids whether from north America, Europe, Siberia, China, Japan or even Australia.

The second factor to consider is the chemical nature of the soil, especially regarding its pH. Many native orchids are either strictly calcicoles (chalk or limestone loving) or calcifuges (chalk or limestone hating) and if your garden is on the chalk or on the acid sands there will be many species you will not be able to grow at all. Nevertheless there are many fairly tolerant species which can live in many different habitats, e.g. *Listera ovata*, *Dactylorhiza fuchsii*, *Epipactis helleborine* and *Gymnadenia conopsea*.

Basically the main orchid habitats are as follows:
Calcareous grasslands on which perhaps the greatest number of species are found.
Neutral grasslands, often clayey cultivated fields, bear certain species in profusion.
Acrd grattlands and **heats** with their specialized vegetation possess many orchids.
Wet acid bogs and **sphagnum moors** with many common and very rare species.
Calcareous woodlands, e.g. beech woods, in which often almost the only ground vegetation is orchids.
Neutral clayey woodlands, e.g. oak woods, with several species in profusion.
Acid woodlands, e.g. pine woods, in which many of the rarer species occur.
Swamp woodlands, e.g. 'carr', in which many orchids are found among the very lush vegetation.

Species confined to any one of these habitats can, obviously, only be grown if these conditions can be re-created. In some instances it is relatively easy to create a piece of calcareous grassland in a garden but to maintain a sphagnum dominated bog at the correct pH and water-level would be a self-defeating exercise. This pH,

183

unfortunately, is very important, as mentioned before. The tolerance ranges of certain species can be from pH 7–8.5 (neutral–alkaline), others tolerate pH 5.5–7 (moderately acid–neutral) but only a few demand a very acid pH 3.5–5.5. With the examples given before the pH ranges of two of the species is as follows: *Gymnadenia conopsea* pH 7–8, *Epipactis helleborine* pH 4.5–8. Other figures are *Ophrys muscifera* pH 6.5–8, and *Dactylrhiza majalis* pH 5.5–8.

Propagation

It is difficult to propagate many temperate region orchids by division because all the root tubers of any single plant are necessary for its well-being. However, rhizomatous species such as *Cypripedium calceolus* have been multiplied by cutting the rhizome into short lengths and then planting these pieces in a sheltered position in the garden in a mixture of sphagnum, nylon fibres and clay. These pieces rooted within ten months and flowers first appeared after two years. It is quite impossible to carry this out commercially but the method should be noted for possible use when propagating some of our rarest species to save them from the danger of extinction.

One might think that temperate orchids could be propagated from seed collected in the wild and this would then enable unlimited numbers to be produced, possibly saving many of our rarer species from extinction. As we have seen in earlier chapters the propagation of tropical orchids from seed is at a very advanced stage but, unfortunately, no such similar spectacular successes have been achieved with temperate orchids. Although the process of germinating these orchid seeds is relatively simple, their being treated in exactly the same manner as tropical ones, the subsequent growing on is very difficult and with certain species has so far proved impossible. However, better final results are sometimes gained by sowing the seeds around the base of already established orchid plants growing in the wild or established in the garden. In these conditions germination failures will be great but seedling establishment will be enhanced probably because the correct symbiotic fungi are present. According to Ziegenspeck, the period between germination and flowering of European native orchids was a very lengthy one. He felt that as the seeds were so small, with little or no room for food reserves, their initial growth would be very slow indeed. This is true, and nothing resembling an ordinary looking seedling is visible for perhaps almost a year. However, after this stage, growth is more rapid and cases have been mentioned of certain species reaching the flowering state, from seed, in no more than three years.

There now follows a synopsis of temperate European, Mediterranean and north American native species, listing those that have either been successfully grown in the past or are well worth experimenting with.

LIST OF ORCHIDS FOR GARDEN CULTIVATION

Aceras anthropophorum
Amerorchis rotundifolia
Anacamptis pyramidalis
Aplectrum hyemale
Arethusa bulbosa
Barlia longibracteata
Blephariglottis alba
Blephariglottis ciliaris
Blephariglottis cristata
Blephariglottis lacera
Blephariglottis leucophaea
Blephariglottis paramoena
Blephariglottis psycodes
Calopogon barbatus
Calopogon multiflorus
Calopogon pallidus
Calopogon pulchellus
Calypso bulbosa
Cephalanthera austinae
Cephalanthera cucullata
Cephalanthera damasonium
Cephalanthera longifolia
Cephalanthera rubra
Chamorchis alpina
Cleistes divaricata
Coeloglossum viride
Criosanthes arietinum
Cypripedium acaule
Cypripedium calceolus
Cypripedium fasciculatum
Cypripedium macranthon
Cypripedium passerinum
Cypripedium reginae
Dactylorhiza cataonica
Dactylorhiza cilicica
Dactylorhiza cordigera
Dactylorhiza cristata

Dactylorhiza cruenta
Dactylorhiza elata
Dactylorhiza foliosa
Dactylorhiza fuchsii
Dactylorhiza incarnata
Dactylorhiza maculata
Dactylorhiza majalis
Dactylorhiza praetermissa
Dactylorhiza purpurella
Dactylorhiza romana
Dactylorhiza russowii
Dactylorhiza sambucina
Epipactis atrorubens
Epipactis dunensis
Epipactis gigantea
Epipactis helleborine
Epipactis leptochila
Epipactis microphylla
Epipactis muelleri
Epipactis palustris
Epipactis phyllanthes
Epipactis purpurata
Galearis spectabilis
Gennaria diphylla
Goodyera oblongifolia
Goodyera pubescens
Goodyera repens
Goodyera tesselata
Gymnadenia conopsea
Gymnadenia odoratissima
Gymnadeniopsis clavellata
Gymnadeniopsis integra
Gymnadeniopsis nivea
Habenaria quinqueseta
Habenaria repens
Herminium monorchis
Hexalectris spicata

Himantoglossum hircinum
Isotria medeoloides
Isotria verticillata
Liparis liliifolia
Liparis loeselii
Listera auriculata
Listera australis
Listera borealis
Listera caurina
Listera convallarioides
Listera cordata
Listera ovata
Listera smallii
Malaxis monophyllos
Malaxis paludosa
Malaxis unifolia
Neotinea intacta
Nigritella nigra
Nigritella rubra
Ophrys apifera
Ophrys arachnitiformis
Ophrys argolica
Ophrys attica
Ophrys bertolonii
Ophrys bombyliflora

Ophrys bornmuelleri
Ophrys cornuta
Ophrys exaltata
Ophrys ferrum-equinum
Ophrys fuciflora
Ophrys fusca
Ophrys lunulata
Ophrys lutea
Ophrys muscifera
Ophrys oxyrrhynchos
Ophrys scolopax
Ophrys speculum
Ophrys sphegodes
Ophrys spruneri
Ophrys tenthredinifera
Orchis anatolica
Orchis collina
Orchis comperana
Orchis coriophora
Orchis italica
Orchis lactea
Orchis laxiflora
Orchis longicornu
Orchis mascula
Orchis militaris

LIST OF ARTIFICIALLY-PRODUCED HYBRID ORCHID GENERA

Only names currently accepted by the Registrar of Orchid Hybrids, and of which plants are known to exist, are given, and all synonyms are omitted.

Acampe × Vanda = Vancampe
Ada × Brassia = Brassada
Ada × Cochlioda = Adioda
Ada × Odontoglossum = Adaglossum
Aërangis × Aëranthes = Thesaëra
Aërides × Arachnis = Aëridachnis
Aërides × Arachnis × Renanthera = Lymanara
Aërides × Arachnis × Ascocentrum × Vanda = Lewisara
Aërides × Arachnus × Vanda = Burkillara
Aërides × Ascocentrum = Aëridocentrum
Aërides × Ascocentrum × Vanda = Christieara
Aërides × Ascoglossum = Aëridoglossum
Aërides × Neofinetia = Aëridofinetia
Aërides × Phalaenopsis = Aëridopsis
Aërides × Phalaenopsis × Vanda = Phalaërianda
Aërides × Renanthera = Renades
Aërides × Renanthera × Vanda = Nobleara
Aërides × Renanthera × Vandopis = Carterara
Aërides × Rhynchostylis = Rhynchorides
Aërides × Rhynchostylis × Vanda = Perreiraara
Aërides × Vanda = Aëridovanda
Aërides × Vandopsis = Vandopsides
Aganisia × Otostylis = Otonisia
Anguloa × Lycaste = Angulocaste
Anoectochilus × Haemaria = Anoectomaria
Ansellia × Cymbidium = Ansidium
Arachnis × Armodorum = Armodachnis
Arachnis × Armodorum × Renanthera = Renaradarum
Arachnis × Ascocentrum = Ascorachnis
Arachnis × Ascocentrum × Vanda = Makara
Arachnis × Phalaenopsis = Arachnopsis
Arachnis × Phalaenopsis × Renanthera = Sappanara
Arachnis × Phalaenopsis × Vanda = Trevorara

Arachnis × Phalaenopsis × Vandopsis = Laycockara
Arachnis × Renanthera = Aranthera
Arachnis × Renanthera × Vanda = Holttumara
Arachnis × Renanthera × Vanda × Vandopsis = Teohara
Arachnis × Renanthera × Vandopsis = Limara
Arachnis × Rhynchostylis = Arachnostylis
Arachnis × Trichoglottis = Arachnoglottis
Arachnis × Trichoglottis × Vanda = Ridleyara
Arachnis × Vanda = Aranda
Arachnis × Vandopsis = Vandachnis
Ascocentrum × Doritis = Doricentrum
Ascocentrum × Doritis × Phalaenopsis = Beardara
Ascocentrum × Doritis × Vanda = Ascovandoritis
Ascocentrum × Ascoglossum × Renanthera × Vanda = Shigeuroara
Ascocentrum × Neofinetia = Ascofinetia
Ascocentrum × Neofinetia × Rhynchostylis = Rumrillara
Ascocentrum × Neofinetia × Vanda = Nakamotoara
Ascocentrum × Phalaenopsis = Asconopsis
Ascocentrum × Phaiaenopsis × Vanda = Deurereukera
Ascocentrum × Renanthera = Renancentrum
Ascocentrum × Renanthera × Vanda = Kagawara
Ascocentrum × Renanthera × Vanda × Vandopsis = Onoara
Ascocentrum × Renantherella = Ascorella
Ascocentrum × Rhynchostylis = Rhynchocentrum
Ascocentrum × Rhynchostylis × Vanda = Vascostylis
Ascocentrum × Sarcohilus = Sarcocentrum
Ascocentrum × Vanda = Ascocenda
Ascoglossum × Renanthera = Renanthoglossum
Ascoglossum × Vanda = Vanglossum
Aspasia × Brassia = Brapasia
Aspasia × Miltonia = Milpasia
Aspasia × Miltonia × Odontoglossum × Oncidium = Withnerara
Aspasia × Odontoglossum = Aspoglossum
Aspasia × Oncidium = Aspasium

Barkeria × Cattleya × Laelia = Laeliocattkeria
Barkeria × Epidendrum = Bardendrum
Barkeria × Laelia = Laeliokeria
Batemannia × Otostylis = Bateostylis

Batemannia × Zygopetalum = Zygobatemannia
Bifrenaria × Lycaste = Lycasteria
Bollea × Chondrorhyncha = Chondrobollea
Bollea × Pescatorea = Pescatobollea
Brassavola × Broughtonia = Brassatonia
Brassavola × Cattleya = Brassocattleya
Brassavola × Cattleya × Diacrium = Hookerara
Brassavola × Cattleya × Diacrium × Laelia = Iwanagara
Brassavola × Cattleya × Epidendrum = Vaughnara
Brassavola × Cattleya × Epidendrum × Laelia = Yamadara
Brassavola × Cattleya × Epidendrum × Laelia × Sophronitis
    = Rothara
Brassavola × Cattleya × Laelia = Brassolaeliocattleya
Brassavola × Cattleya × Laelia × Schomburgkia = Recchara
Brassavola × Cattleya × Laelia × Sophronitis = Potinara
Brassavola × Cattleya × Laeliopsis = Fujiwarara
Brassavola × Cattleya × Schomburgkia = Dekensara
Brassavola × Cattleya × Sophronitis = Rolfeara
Brassavola × Diacrium = Brassodiacrium
Brassavola × Epidendrum = Brassoepidendrum
Brassavola × Laelia = Brassolaelia
Brassavola × Laelia × Sophronitis = Lowara
Brassavola × Rhyncholaelia = Rhynchovola
Brassavola × Schomburgkia = Schombavola
Brassavola × Sophronitis = Brassaphronitis
Brassia × Chochlioda × Miltonia × Odontoglossum = Beallara
Brassia × Cochlioda × Odontoglossum = Sanderara
Brassia × Miltonia = Miltassia
Brassia × Miltonia × Odontoglossum = Degarmoara
Brassia × Miltonia × Oncidium = Aliceara
Brassia × Odontoglossum = Odontobrassia
Brassia × Oncidium = Brassidium
Brassia × Rodriguezia = Rodrassia
Broughtonia × Brassavola = Brassatonia
Broughtonia × Cattleya = Cattleytonia
Broughtonia × Cattleya × Laelia = Laeliocatonia
Broughtonia × Cattleya × Laeliopsis = Osmentara
Broughtonia × Cattleyopsis = Cattleyopsistonia
Broughtonia × Cattleyopsis × Laeliopsis = Gauntlettara

189

Broughtonia × Diacrium = Diabroughtonia
Broughtonia × Diacrium × Schomburgkia = Shipmanara
Broughtonia × Domingoa = Domintonia
Broughtonia × Epidendrum = Epitonia
Broughtonia × Epidendrum × Laeliopsis = Moscosoara
Broughtonia × Laelia = Laelonia
Broughtonia × Laelia × Sophronitis = Hartara
Broughtonia × Laeliopsis = Lioponia
Broughtonia × Laeliopsis × Tetramiera = Bloomara
Broughtonia × Schomburgkia = Schombonia
Broughtonia × Sophronitis = Sophrobroughtonia
Broughtonia × Tetramicra = Tetratonia

Calanthe × Gastrorchis = Gastrocalanthe
Calanthe × Phaius = Phaiocalanthe
Catasetum × Cycnoches = Catanoches
Catasetum × Mormodes = Catamodes
Cattleya × Cattleyopsis × Epidendrum = Hawkesara
Cattleya × Diacrium = Diacattleya
Cattleya × Diacrium × Laelia = Dialaeliocattleya
Cattleya × Diacrium × Schomburgkia = Mizutara
Cattleya × Domingioa × Epidendrum = Arizara
Cattleya × Epidendrum = Epicattleya
Cattleya × Epidendrum × Laelia = Epilaeliocattleya
Cattleya × Epidendrum × Laelia × Sophronitis = Kirchara
Cattleya × Laelia = Laeliocattleya
Cattleya × Laelia × Schomburgkia = Lyonara (1959)
Cattleya × Laelia × Schomburgkia × Sophronitis = Herbertara
Cattleya × Laelia × Sophronitis = Sophrolaeliocattleya
Cattleya × Laeliopsis = Laeliopleya
Cattleya × Schomburgkia = Schombocattleya
Cattleya × Sophronitis = Sophrocattleya
Cattleyopsis × Domingoa = Cattleyopsisgoa
Chondrorhyncha × Zygopetalum = Zygorhyncha
Cochleanthes × Huntleya = Huntleanthes
Cochleanthes × Pescatorea = Pescoranthes
Cochleanthes × Stenia = Cochlenia
Cochlioda × Miltonia = Miltonioda
Cochlioda × Miltonia × Odontoglossum = Vuylstekeara

190

Cochlioda × Miltonia × Odontoglossum × Oncidium = Burrageara
Cochlioda × Miltonia × Oncidium = Charlesworthara
Cochlioda × Odontoglossum = Odontioda
Cochlioda × Odontoglossum × Oncidium = Wilsonara
Cochlioda × Oncidium = Oncidioda
Colax × Zygopetalum = Zygocolax
Comparettia × Ionopsis = Ionettia
Comparettia × Oncidium = Oncidettia
Comparettia × Oncidium × Rodriguezia = Warneara
Comparettia × Rodriguezia = Rodrettia
Cycnoches × Mormodes = Cycnodes
Cymbidium × Grammatophyllum = Grammatocymbidium
Cymbidium × Phaius = Phaiocymbidium

Diacrium × Epidendrum = Epidiacrium
Diacrium × Laelia = Dialaelia
Diacrium × Laeliopsis = Dialaeliopsis
Diacrium × Schomburgkia = Diaschomburgkia
Domingoa × Epidendrum = Epigoa
Domingoa × Hexadesmia = Domindesmia
Domingoa × Laeliopsis = Domliopsis
Doritis × Kingiella = Doriella
Doritis × Kingiella × Phalaenopsis = Doriellaopsis
Doritis × Phalaenopsis = Doritaenopsis
Doritis × Phalaenopsis × Rhynchostylis = Rhyndoropsis
Doritis × Vanda = Vandoritis
Dossinia × Haemaria = Dossinimaria

Epidendrum × Laelia = Epilaelia
Epidendrum × Laelia × Schomburgkia = Dillonara
Epidendrum × Laelia × Sophronitis = Stanfieldara
Epidendrum × Laeliopsis = Epilaeliopsis
Epidendrum × Schomburgkia = Schomboepidendrum
Epidendrum × Sophronitis = Epiphronitis

Gastrorkis × Phaius = Gastrophaius
Gomesa × Macradenia = Macradesa
Gomesa × Oncidium = Oncidesa

Habenaria × Pecteilis = Pectabenaria
Haemaria × Macodes = Macomaria

Ionopsis × Oncidium = Ionocidium
Ionopsis × Rodriguezia = Rodriopsis

Laelia × Laeliopsis = Liaopsis
Laelia × Leptotes = Leptolaelia
Laelia × Schomburgkia = Schombolaelia
Laelia × Sophronitis = Sophrolaelia
Laeliopsis × Tetramicra = Tetraliopsis
Luisia × Vanda = Luisanda
Lycaste × Zygopetalum = Zygocaste

Macradenia × Oncidium = Oncidenia
Macradenia × Rodriguezia = Rodridenia
Mendoncella × Zygopetalum = Zygocella
Miltonia × Ondontoglossum = Odontonia
Miltonia × Odontoglossum × Oncidium = Colmanara
Miltonia × Oncidium = Miltonidium
Miltonia × Rodriguezia = Rodritonia
Miltonia × Trichopilia = Milpilia

Neofinetia × Phalaenopsis = Phalaenetia
Neofinetia × Renanthera = Renanetia
Neofinetia × Rhynchostylis = Neostylis
Neofinetia × Vanda = Vandofinetia

Odontoglossum × Oncidium = Odontocidium
Oncidium × Ornithophora = Ornitpocidium
Oncidium × Rodriguezia = Rodricidium
Oncidium × Trichocentrum = Trichocidium
Oncidium × Trichopilia = Oncidpilia
Otostylis × Zygopetalum = Zygostylis
Otostylis × Zygosepalum = Otosepalum

Paphiopedilum × Phragmipedium = Phragmipaphium
Phalaenopsis × Renanthera = Renanthopsis
Phalaenopsis × Renanthera × Vanda = Moirara

Phalaenopsis × Rhynchostylis = Rhynchonopsis
Phalaenopsis × Rhynchostylis × Vanda = Yapara
Phalaenopsis × Sarochilus = Saronopsis
Phalaenopsis × Vanda = Vandaenopsis
Phalaenopsis × Vandopsis = Phalandopsis

Renanthera × Renantherella = Ellanthera
Renanthera × Rhynchostylis = Renanstylis
Renanthera × Sarcochilus = Sarcothera
Renanthera × Trichoglottis = Renaglottis
Renanthera × Vanda = Renantanda
Renanthera × Vanda × Vandopsis = Hawaiiara
Renanthera × Vandopsis = Renanopsis
Rhinerrhiza × Sarcochilus = Sarcorhiza
Rhynchostylis × Vanda = **Rhynchovanda**
Rhynchostylis × Vandopsis = Opsistylis

Sarochilus × Vanda = Sarcovanda
Schomburgkia × Sophronitis = Schombonitis

Trichoglottis × Vanda = Trichovanda
Trichoglottis × Vandopsis = Trichopsis

Vanda × Vandopsis = Opsisanda

SELECTED NORTH AMERICAN TERRESTRIAL
ORCHIDACEAE OF HORTICULTURAL INTEREST

This appendix has been specially compiled by Professor de Tomasi, for North American readers who may find that some of these species will possibly survive in cultivation. However, several of them are only from the sub-tropical parts of the USA (e.g. *Spiranthes orchioides*, *Eulophia alta*) and, therefore, will not be suitable for cultivation away from these areas; likewise some others require very specialized soil conditions and may prove difficult to establish.

Name	Flower	Habitat	Geographical Distribution
Aplectrum hyemale	yellowish to white, purple spotted; lip whitish purple spotted, crinkly edged May–June	moist woodlands, bogs, larch swamps 0–1300 m	Quebec to Saskatchewan ; south to Georgia, Alabama, Arkansas, Arizona
Arethusa bulbosa	pink to magenta; lip yellow and pink; lip disk fleshy-bearded May–August	sphagnum bogs, wet meadows 0–1200 m	Newfoundland to Minnesota; south to the Carolinas, Midwest
Bletia purpurea	white, rose or deep purple; lip trilobed Primarily November–June occasionally all year	damp marls, pinelands swamps, watery woods, humid rocky ledges 0–1200 m	South Florida. Also: Bahamas, West Indies, central and north South America
Calopogon pulchellus	white to magenta; lip disc purply-yellow, fleshy-bearded March–August	acid meadows, cranberry bogs, wet woods 0–1000 m	Newfoundland to Minnesota; south to Florida, Texas, Arkansas. Also: Bahamas, Cuba
Calypso bulbosa	green-purple to white; lip red-maroon inside, whitish outside with three yellow-brown hairy ridges April–July	moist woodlands, bogs, larch swamps 0–1300 m	Labrador to British Columbia, Alaska, Aleutians; south to north. New York, Michigan, Colorado, N. Arizona and California Also: Eurasia
Cleistes divaricata	purple to white, dark veins; sepals brownish April–July	moist pine barrens, gulches, savannahs swamps 0–1300 m	New Jersey, Tennessee; south to Florida, East Texas
Corallorhiza maculata	sepals and petals green-purple; lip white, purple-spotted April–September	rich humus, moist forest floor 0–3500 m	Newfoundland to Alberta, British Columbia; south to N. Carolina, Texas. Arizona, Pacific states Also: Mexico, Guatemala
Cypripedium acaule	sepals and petals green-brown; lip pouch pink to reddish, veined occasionally white April–July	moderate shade, acid light humus, bogs 0–1600 m	Arctic Circle (N.W. Canada) to Georgia mountains

Name	Flower	Habitat	Geographical Distribution
Cypripedium arietinum (Criosanthes arietinum)	sepals and petals green-brown to reddish; lip pouch with white woolly mouth, starkly veined May–June	bogs, swamps, evergreen areas, dry high forest 0–4000 m	Quebec, Ontario to Minnesota; south to central New York. Also: W. China
Cypripedium calceolus	sepals and petals yellow to brown purple; lip pouch cream to gold-yellow April–August	humid meadows and woods 0–2700 m	Newfoundland to Yukon; south to Gulf states (mountains), Asia. Also: Europe
Cypripedium californicum	sepals brown-yellow; petals yellow; lip white-pink, pouch veined May–July	western damp woods, stream banks 200–1800 m	California, Oregon
Cypripedium candidum	sepals green-yellow, spotted; petals yellowish, lip pouch white, shiny, veined and hairy within April–June	bogs in grasslands wet woods on limestone, marls 100–1500 m	Ontario to Minnesota; south to Kentucky
Cypripedium fasciculatum	sepals and petals yellow to purple, veined; lip pouch yellowish April–August	western evergreen mountain forest 300–2500 m	Montana, Washington, Colorado, California
Cypripedium guttatum	white, purple spots; lip pouch hairy within June–August	western open woods, grasslands 0–4000 m	British Columbia, Yukon, Alaska, Aleutians. Also: Siberia, China to central Russia
Cypripedium montanum	sepals and petals green-purplish; lip pouch white and purple, hairy within May–July	western sub-alpine woods 300–1800 m	Alberta, British Columbia; south to Wyoming, California
Cypripedium passerinum	sepals yellow-green; petals white; lip pouch, translucent, white to pink, purple marked inside and out June–July	far north, littoral gravels and sands, coniferous humus 0–2200 m	Arctic Circle; south to British Columbia; east to Quebec
Cypripedium reginae	sepals and petals white; lip pouch white; pink, to crimson in mouth region, pink veined May–August	evergreen and meadow bogs, low acidity soils 100–1500 m	Newfoundland to Saskatchewan; south to Ohio, Alabama. Also: W. China

195

Name	Flower	Habitat	Geographical Distribution
Eulophia alta	green-bronze; lip darker with purple streaks May, September to December	rich humus, acid soils, hammocks and ponds 0–1200 m	South Florida. Also: West Indies and Trinidad, central and north South America, Africa
Epipactis gigantea	sepals and petals green to pink red nerves; lip purple-red veined March–August	shady, wet or marshy areas, limestone outcrops 0–2700 m	South Dakota, British Columbia; south to New Mexico, Texas
Epipactis helleborine (foreign introduction)	green-purplish with white and red June–September	moist rocky woods, roadsides 100–600 m	Quebec to Montana; south to Penn., Missouri. Introduced from Europe
Galeandra beyrichii	yellow-green; lip whitish and purple streaks July–December	wet forest, roadsides hammocks 0–1200 m	Florida. Also: W. Indies, Costa Rica, north South America
Goodyera pubescens	white May–October	semi-dry coniferous or mixed forest, moist uplands rhododendron-laurel thickets 0–1500 m	Quebec to Minnesota; Iowa; south to Georgia Alabama
Habenaria blephariglottis (Blephariglottis alba)	white or cream June–September	sandy, acid bogs, sphagnum and cranberry areas, barrens, upland meadows 0–700 m	Newfoundland to Michigan; south to coastal plains, Florida, Texas
Habenaria ciliaris (Blephariglottis ciliaris)	similar to *H. Blephariglottis alba*, yellow to orange June–September	ubiquitous, acid, wet and dry wooded or grassy locations 0–1800 m	similar to *H. blephariglottis*
Habenaria cristata (Blephariglottis cristata)	dark yellow-orange June–September	wet pinelands, upland woods and meadows, cypress swamps 0–800 m	New England, south to Florida, Arkansas, Texas
Habenaria dilatata (Platanthera dilatata)	green to white April–September	moist meadows, forests, tidal areas 0–3000 m	Greenland, Labrador to Alaska, Aleutians; south to New Jersey, Pennsylvania, Colorado, Pacific states
Habenaria fimbriata (H. psycodes var. grandiflora) (also Blephariglottis grandiflora)	similar to *Habenaria psycodes* June–August	see *Habenaria psycodes*	see *Habenaria psycodes*
Habenaria flava (Platanthera flava)	yellow-green March–September	wet meadows, bogs, swamps, alluvial areas 0–300 m	Nova Scotia, Minnesota; south to Florida, Texas

Name	Flower	Habitat	Geographical Distribution
Habenaria hookeri (Platanthera hookeri)	yellow-green May–August	open marshes, wet woods and fields 0–1200 m	Nova Scotia to Minn.; south to Pennsylvania; Iowa
Habenaria integra (Gymnadeniopsis integra)	gold-yellow to orange July–September	acid soils, barrens, bogs, swampy areas 0–1000 m	New Jersey; south to central Florida, Gulf Coast, Texas
Habenaria lacera (Blephariglottis lacera)	creamy to yellow-green May–August	open marshes, wet woods, open fields 0–1200 m	Newfoundland to Manitoba; south to Georgia, Arkansas, Texas
Habenaria leucophaea (Blephariglottis leucophaea)	creamy to white May–August	low elevation sphagnum bogs, wet prairie, coniferous woods 0–200 m	Nova Scotia to Dakota; south to New York, Arkansas
Habenaria nivea (Gymnadeniopsis nivea)	white May–September	acid sandy pine barrens, savannahs 0–500 m	New Jersey; south to Florida, Arkansas, Texas
Habenaria obtusata (Platanthera obtusata)	green-white June–September	wet coniferous forest muskegs, stream banks 100–3500 m	Labrador to Alaska, Aleutians; south to north New York, Minn., Montana, Colorado. Also: Norway
Habenaria orbiculata (Platanthera orbiculata) (also: H. macrophylla)	green-white June–September	moderately moist, evergreen or mixed forest 100–1800 m	Labrador to Alaska, Aleutians; south to N. Carolina, Georgia mountains; west to Montana, Oregon, Washington
Habenaria paramoena (Blephariglottis paramoena)	bright pink-purple June–September	moist woods and grasslands 100–900 m	West, New York, Penn., Missouri; south to Georgia, Arkansas
Habenaria psycodes (Blephariglottis psycodes)	white to lilac-purple June–August	swampy woods, stream beds, upland meadows, sandy northern beaches 0–2200 m	Newfoundland to Minn.; south to Georgia mountains, Arkansas
Habenaria quinqueseta	green-white August–January	low hardwoods, pinelands, moist grasslands 0–2200 m	South Carolina; south to Florida, Gulf Coast Texas. Also: Caribbean, central America
Habenaria viridis (Coeloglossum viride) also: var. H. bracteata	green, occasionally red-purple-brown tinge on column, lip spur whitish or reddish May–August	moist coniferous mixed woods, meadows, bogs grasslands, sand dunes etc. 0–2700 m	Newfoundland to British Columbia, Alaska, Aleutians; south to N. Carolina mountains; west to New Mexico, Utah, Washington. Also: Europe

197

Name	Flower	Habitat	Geographical Distribution
Hexalectris spicata	yellow-buff with dark streaks; sepals and petals, purple-brown; lip creamy-white with violet-purple striations June–September	shell-coral marls rich humus, humid coniferous and hardwood limestone forests 0–2300 m	Maryland to Missouri, south to Florida Gulf Coast, Arkansas, Texas, Arizona. Also: Mexico
Isotria verticillata	green-purple May–August	pine and hardwoods, damp, rich humus, bogs 0–1000 m	New England to Missouri; south to North Florida, Arkansas, Texas
Liparis liliifolia	mauve-lavender; sepals green-white translucent, petals mauve to purple; lip purple-veined, shiny median May–July	mossy locations in woods, thickets, ravines 0–1700 m	Maine to Minn.; south to Georgia, Arkansas Also: China
Liparis loeselii	green-white May–August	damp evergreen forests, wet meadows, bogs fens, sand-dunes 0–1200 m	Nova Scotia to Manitoba Washington south to North Carolina, Alabama, Europe
Listera auriculata	white-green, purple tinged June–August	mossy alluvial soils, woods, swamps low elevations	Newfoundland; south to New Hampshire, New York, Michigan
Listera australis	red-purple; lip deep crimson with green central ridge February–July	damp woods, sphagnum patches, brush thickets, bogs low elevations	Quebec, Ontario; south to central Florida, Texas
Listera borealis	pale yellow-green, dark green veined; lip translucent March–July	mossy coniferous and mixed woods, swampy edges 0–3000 m	St Lawrence, Hudson Bay to Alaska; south to Utah, Colorado
Listera convallarioides	yellow-green June–September	humid coniferous and mixed woods, moss and leaf moulds, bogs 100–2600 m	Newfoundland to Alaska; south to Carolina mountains, Michigan, Arizona, Pacific states
Listera reniformis (L. smallii)	white-green; lip white-veined June–July	hemlock, rhododendron and other shady humid forest 500–1800 m	Pennsylvania, south to Georgia and Tennessee mountains. Also: Asia
Orchis rotundifolia (Amerorchis rotundifolia)	white-pinkish-mauve; lip white and purple spots March–August	northern limestone forest, mossy swamps 100–1200 m	Greenland, Alaska; south to north. New England, Wyoming; Montana
Orchis spectabilis (Galearis spectabilis)	pink to mauve-purple; lip white April–July	mildly acid woodlands, alluvial soils 100–1500 m	Quebec to Minn.; south to Alabama, Arkansas

Name	Flower	Habitat	Geographical Distribution
Pogonia ophioglossoides	white to pink; lip with dark veins, yellow-white bearded crest March–August	bogs, muskegs, wet meadows, open woods in sedges and moss 0–800 m	Newfoundland to Minn.; south to Florida, Texas
Spiranthes cernua (Also: var. odorata)	white July–December	meadows, bogs, wet woods, barrens, dunes 0–1800	Nova Scotia to Minn.; Nebraska; south to Florida, Texas
Spiranthes cinnabarina (Stenorrhynchus cinnabarina)	orange to saffron July–October	dry, grassy calcareous mountains 1000–2500 m	Texas. Also: Mexico, Guatemala
Spiranthes orchioides (Stenorrhynchus orchioides)	cream to dark vermilion March–August	damp soils, bogs, dry grasslands 0–2800 m	Florida. Also: Caribbean, Mexico, central and south America
Spiranthes romanzoffiana	cream-white July–October	moist locations in fields, open woods 500–3000 m	Newfoundland to Alaska; Aleutians; south to Pacific states and south-west. Also: British Isles
Spiranthes vernalis	cream-white, reddish-fuzzy January–August	wet meadows, salt marshes, deciduous and evergreen woods 0–3000 m	Quebec to Neb; south to Fla., Texas, Okla., New Mexico. Also: Mexico Guatemala
Triphora trianthophora	white to pink disc with three green ridges July–October	rich humus, leafmould, decaying wood 0–3000 m	New England to Wisconsin; south to central Florida, Texas. Also: Mexico Guatemala, Panama
Zeuxine strateumatica (foreign introduction)	white, shiny; lip yellow January–February	grassy open areas along ditches, lawns 0–1000 m	weedy introduction from Far East: Florida, Gulf Coast. Also: North central Asia, China, Japan, Philippines, India, Indonesia

ORCHID NURSERYMEN IN BRITAIN

Armstrong and Brown, Orchidhurst, Liptraps Lane, Tunbridge Wells, Kent
Black and Flory Ltd, Middle Green, Slough, Bucks
Burnham Nurseries Ltd, Orchid Avenue, Kingsteignton, Newton Abbot, Devon
Carnosa Plants, Cedar Orchid Nursery, Wash Lane, South Mimms, Herts
Charlesworth and Co. Ltd, Haywards Heath, Sussex
Dell Park Orchid Nursery, Englefield Green, Egham, Surrey
Harry Dixon and Sons, Spencer Park Nursery, Wandsworth Common. London
   SW 18
Jeal's Nurseries (Fernhill) Ltd, Fernhill Road, Horley, Surrey
Keith Andrews Orchids Ltd, Plush, Dorchester, Dorset
A. J. Keeling and Sons, Grange Nurseries, Westgate Hill, Bradford, Yorkshire
Stuart Low (Benenden) Ltd, Jarvis Brook, Crowborough, Sussex
McBean's Orchids Ltd, Cooksbridge, Lewes, Sussex
Mansell and Hatcher Ltd, Cragg Wood Nurseries, Rawden, Leeds
Neville Orchids, Baltonsborough, Glastonbury, Somerset
R. and E. Ratcliffe, Downland Nurseries, Chilton, Didcot, Berks
Stonehurst Orchid Laboratories, Ardingly, Haywards Heath, Sussex
Wyld Court Orchids, Hampstead Norris, Newbury, Berks

BRITISH ORCHID SOCIETIES

(for current addresses see latest issues of *Orchid Review* etc.)

Birmingham and Midland Orchid Society
Bournemouth, Poole and District Orchid Society
Bristol and West of England Orchid Society
Cambridge and District Orchid Society
Central Orchid Society
Cheshire and North Wales Orchid Society
Devon and Cornwall Orchid Society
Manchester and North of England Orchid Society
Medway and District Discussion Group (of OSGB)
Orchid Society of East Anglia
Orchid Society of Great Britain
Scottish Orchid Society
Solihull and District Orchid Society
South Wales and Monmouthshire Orchid Society
Thames Valley Orchid Society

SELECTED LIST OF MAJOR USA ORCHID NURSERIES

Alberts and Merkel Bros, PO Box 537 AM, Boynton Beach, Florida 33435
Dos Pueblos Orchid Company, PO Box 158, Goleta, California 93017
Arthur Freed Orchids, 5731 South Bonsall Drive, Malibu, California 90265
Herb. Hager, Box 544, Santa Cruz, California 95060
Jones and Scully, Orchidglade, 2200 NW 33rd Avenua, Miami, Florida 33142
Wm Kirch-Orchids Ltd, 2630 Waiomao Road, Honolulu, Hawaii 96816
Oscar M. Kirsch, 2869 Oahu Avenue, Honolulu, Hawaii 96822
Lager and Hurrell, 426 Morris Avenua, Summit, New Jersey 07901
Rivermont Orchids, PO Box 67, Signal Mountain, Tennessee 37377
Riverview Orchids, East Liverpool, Ohio 43920
Rod McLellan Co., 1450 El Camino Real, South San Francisco, California 94080
Santa Barbara Orchid Estate, 1250 Orchid Drive, Santa Barbara, California 93105
Schaffer's Tropical Gardens, 1220 41st Avenue, Santa Cruz, California 95060
Fred. A. Stewart, 1212 East Las Turas Drive, San Gabriel, California 91778

SELECTED LIST OF MAJOR ORCHID NURSERIES OUTSIDE BRITAIN AND USA

AUSTRALIA
Adelaide Orchids, 23 Creslin Terrace, Camden Park, South Australia 5034
Gold Coast Orchids, 14 Brake Street, Burleigh Heads, Queensland 4220
Slattery's Nursery, 12 Eddystone Road, Bexley, New South Wales 2207
Wondabah Orchids, 724 Pennant Hills Road, Carlingford, New South Wales 2118
West Coast Orchids, 100 Spring Road, Thornlie, West Australia 6108

BRAZIL
Orquidearia Catarinense, PO Box 1, Corupa, Santa Catarina

FINLAND
Kapparberg Orchids, Nådendal

FRANCE
Marcel Lecoufle, 5 rue de Paris, 94, Boissy-St-Léger, Val de Marne
Maurice Vacherot, 31 rue de Valenton, 94, Boissy-St-Léger, Val de Marne
Vacherot and Lecoufle, La Tuilerie, BP 8, 94, Boissy-St-Léger, Val de Marne

GERMAN FEDERAL REPUBLIC
H. Wickman, 31 Celle 2, Bahnhofstraße 34
Erika Reuter, 2844, Lemförde, Hannover

INDIA
G. Ghose & Co., Townend, Darjeeling
Ganesh Mani Pradhan, Ganesh Villa, Kalimpong

JAPAN
Fuji Nurseries, PO Box 43, Kurashiki 710

JAVA
A. Kalopaking, D J L Pungkurago 1, Lawang, East Java

NEW ZEALAND
A. Beck, Ngatea, RD, Havraki Plains

PHILIPPINES
Bayanihan Orchids, PO Box 4218, Manila

SINGAPORE
Holland Nursery, $4^1/_4$ ms, Holland Road, Singapore 10
Koh Keng Hoe Orchid Nursery, 8 Adam Road, Singapore 11
Seng Heng Orchid Nursery, 87-P, Stagmont Ring, Singapore 11
Singapore Orchids, 337 Thomsa Road, Singapore 11
Sun Kee Orchid Nursery, 57 A Lorong Bundul, Singapore 19

SOUTH AFRICA
Paradise Orchids, 10 Bedford Road, Cowies Hill, Natal

SWITZERLAND
E. Gunzenhauser Orchids, 4460 Gelterkinden

TAIWAN
Chow Cheng Orchids, 94 Litoh Street, Taichung

THAILAND
Bangrabue Nursery, 15 Klahom's Lane, PO Box 3–150, Bangkrabuee

NATIONAL ORCHID SOCIETIES AND COUNCILS

(This list does not include trade associations; see American Orchid Society current Yearbook for list of approximately 200 orchid societies in USA and associated territories, Canada, New Zealand etc.)

AUSTRALIA
Australian Orchid Council, 15 Bayview Place, Bayview, NSW 2104
(representing all State orchid societies)

AUSTRIA
Österreichische Orchideen-Gesellschaft, 1020 Vienna, Wientraubengasse 25–27

BAHAMAS
Orchid Society of Bahamas, PO Box 265, Freeport, Grand Bahama Island

BARBADOS
Barbados Orchid Circle, 'The Grotto', River Road, St Michael

BRAZIL
Sociedade Brasileira do Orquidofilos, Caixa Postal 4714, Rio de Janeiro

BRUNEI
Brunei State Orchid Society, c/o Brunei Shell Petroleum Co. Ltd, Seria

CEYLON
Orchid Circle of Ceylon, 22 Barnes Place, Colombo

COLOMBIA
Sociedad Colombiana de Orquideologia, ap. Aereo 4725, Medellin

CZECHOSLOVAKIA
Club der Orchideenfreunde in Prag, Prag XVI, Staropramenni

DENMARK
Dansk Orchide Club, Dyrlaege, 4174, Jystrup, Ndl

FRANCE
Société Francaise d'Orchidophilie, 49, Village de Grasse, 78, Feucherolles

203

GERMANY (FEDERAL REPUBLIC)
Deutsche Orchideen-Gesellschaft E.V., 842 Kelheim Breslauer Str. 20

HAITI
Orchid Society of Haiti, c/o Madsen and Co., Port-au-Prince

HAWAII
Hawaiian Orchid Societies Inc., 84–839 Mena Street, Waianae, Oahu, Hawaii 96792
(representing Hawaiian orchid societies)

HOLLAND
Nederlandse Orchideen Vereniging, Emmastraat 14, Aalsmeer

ITALY
Associazione Italiana per la Orchidee, Via Dante 11, 25100 Brescia

JAMAICA
Jamaica Orchid Sciety, Wai Rua Road, Gorden Town PO, Kingston 7

JAPAN
Japan Orchid Society, 1476 Shironomae, Mikagecho, Higashinadaku, Kobe

KENYA
Kenya Orchid Society, PO Box 241, Nairobi

MALAYSIA AND SINGAPORE
Orchid Society of South East Asia, PO Box 2363, Singapore

MEXICO
Sociedad Orquidofila de Guadalajara, Frias 75, Guadalajara, Jalisco

NEW ZEALAND
New Zealand Orchid Society, 34A Evelyn Place, Northcote, Auckland 10

PERU
Orchid Society of Peru, Jacinto Lara 210, San Isidro, Lima

PHILIPPINES
Philippine Orchid Society, PO Box 1105, Manila

RHODESIA
Rhodesian Orchid Society, PO Box 8196, Causeway, Salisbury

SOUTH AFRICA
South African Orchid Council, P.O. Box 2678, Johannesburg
(representing all South African orchid societies)

SWEDEN
Orchid Club of Stockholm, 124–02, Bandhagen, Kallforsvägen 29

SWITZERLAND
Schweizerische Orchideengesellschaft, CH-8 105, Regensdorf ZH, Püntweg 4

TAIWAN
Taiwan Orchid Society, no. 9–2, Lane 97, Tong An Street, Taipei

THAILAND
Orchid Society of Thailand, North Nakornrajsima Road, Bangkok

TRINIDAD
Trinidad Orchid Society, room 247, Texaco Trinidad, Point-a-Pierre

UNITED KINGDOM
(see separate list, p. 203) British Orchid Council, 28 Felday Road, Lewisham, London SE13

UNITED STATES OF AMERICA
Cymbidium Society of America, 7102 Cole Street, Downey, California 90242
International Phalaenopsis Society of America, PO Box 507, West Palm Beach, Florida 33402
There are over two hundred local societies which are affiliated with The American Orchid Society. For the address of your local chapter, write to: The American Orchid Society, Botanical Museum of Harvard University, Cambridge, Massachusetts 02138

VENEZUELA
Sociedad de Orquideologia de Carabobo, Aptdo. 95, Valencia

SUPPLIERS OF EQUIPMENT
FOR GROWING ORCHIDS (UK ONLY)

Orchid houses

G. F. Strawson and Son, 6 St Andrews Works, Charlesfield Road, Horley, Surrey

C. H. Whitehouse Ltd, Buckhurst Works, Frant, Sussex

(for names and addresses of non-specialist greenhouses suitable for orchid growing see advertisements in weekly and monthly horticultural journals)

Heating, ventilating, watering and shading apparatus

NB Nearly all greenhouse manufacturers and suppliers also sell equipment for heating etc.

British Overhead Irrigation Ltd, Ringwood, Hampshire

Automatic Sunblind Installations, 98 Rushes Road, Petersfield, Hants

Humex Ltd, 5 High Road, Byfleet, Surrey

Metallic Constructions Co. (Derby) Ltd, Bridge Works, Alfreton Road, Derby

Composts

NB Nearly all orchid nurserymen also sell various potting composts.

G. S. Brown, Martletwy, Narberth, Pembrokeshire

Genista Ltd, Farsley, Pudsey, Yorkshire (plastic granules)

Pesticides, insecticides and fungicides

NB Many orchid nurserymen also sell various proprietary brands of pesticides etc.

Murphy Chemical Co. Ltd, Wheathampstead, St Albans, Hertfordshire

USEFUL BOOKS ABOUT ORCHIDS

Commonwealth Mycological Institute *Plant Pathologists' Pocketbook* England, Kew 1968

Darnell, A. W. *Orchids for the Outdoor Garden* England, Ashford 1930

Darwin, C. *On the Various Contrivances by which British and Foreign Orchids are Fertilized by Insects and the Good Effects of Intercrossing* London 1862

Dodson, C. H. and Gillespie, R. *The Biology of the Orchid* USA, Nashville 1967

Holttum, R. E. *Flora of Malaya, vol. 1. Orchids* ed. 3. Singapore 1964

International Orchid Commission *Handbook on Orchid Nomenclature and Registration.* USA, Cambridge 1969

Ministry of Agriculture, Fisheries and Food *Chemicals for the Gardener* ed. 2. London 1965

Northen, R. *Home Orchid Growing* ed.3. USA, Princeton 1962

Proceedings of the Second World Orchid Conference 1957 USA, Cambridge 1958

Proceedings of the Third World Orchid Conference 1960 London 1960

Proceedings of the Fourth World Orchid Conference 1963 Singapore 1966

Proceedings of the Fifth World Orchid Conference 1966 USA, Long Beach 1966

Richter, W. (transl. Launert, E., ed. Hunt, P. F.) *The Orchid World* London 1965

Royal Horticultural Society *Sander's List of Orchid Hybrids: Addendum 1961–1963* London 1964; *Addendum 1964–1966* London 1967, *Addendum 1961–1970* London 1971

Sanders (St Albans) Ltd *Sander's List of Orchid Hybrids 1856–1946* England, St Albans 1949

David Sander's Orchids Ltd *David Sander's One-table List of Orchid Hybrids, 1946–1960* England, Selsfield 1961

Schultes, R. E. and Pease, A. S. *Generic Names of Orchids* New York 1963

Summerhayes, V. S. *Wild Orchids of Britain* ed.2. London 1968

van der Pijl, L. and Dodson, C. H. *Orchid Flowers, their Pollination and Evolution* USA, Coral Gables 1966

Veitch, J. and Sons *Manual of Orchidaceous Plants* London 1887–1894

Williams, B. S. (ed. Williams, H. S.) *The Orchid Growers Manual* ed.7. 1894

Withner, C. L. (ed.) *The Orchids, A Scientific Survey* New York 1959

MAJOR ORCHID PERIODICALS

American Orchid Society Bulletin USA, Cambridge

Australian Orchid Review Australia, Darlinghurst

Cymbidium Society News USA, Santa Paula

Die Orchidee Germany, Hamburg

Journal of the Orchid Society of Great Britain England, St Albans

Malayan Orchid Review Singapore

New Zealand Orchid Review New Zealand, Northcote

Orchadian Australia, Sydney

Orchid Digest USA, La Canada

Orchid Review England, Caterham

Orquidea Brazil, Rio de Janeiro

Orquideologia Colombia, Medellin

Pacific Orchid Society of Hawaii Bulletin Hawaii, Honolulu

INDEX

Page numbers in italics refer to illustrations

Photographs are reproduced by permission of:

Dr. M. Schwabe, Braunschweig-Lehndorf pp. 17, 45, 48/3, 76/1, 85, 88, 97/6, 125/2, 128/1/5/7, 137/4/6/8/9, 156, 165, 168. – Dieter Täuber, Vieselbach pp. 18, 87, 126, 127. – Kuno Krieger, Dortmund-Eving pp. 58/2/3. – Prof. Borris, Greifswald pp. 155/1. – Theodor Haber, Datteln/Westf. pp. 128/6. – Dr. M. Kron, Ebeleben pp. 137/6. – G. E. Nicholson p. 0/1. – The rest by the author